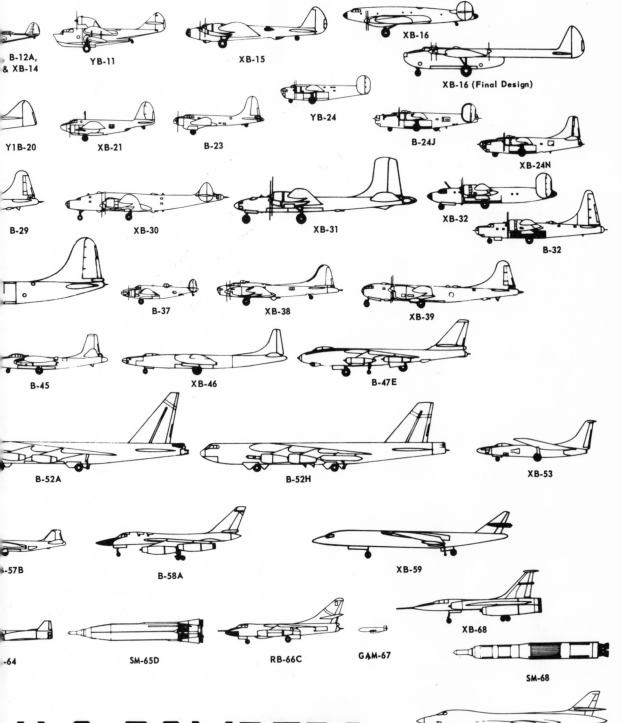

B-12A, & XB-14 — YB-11 — XB-15 — XB-16 — XB-16 (Final Design)

Y1B-20 — XB-21 — B-23 — YB-24 — B-24J — XB-24N

B-29 — XB-30 — XB-31 — XB-32 — B-32

B-37 — XB-38 — XB-39

B-45 — XB-46 — B-47E

B-52A — B-52H — XB-53

-57B — B-58A — XB-59

-64 — SM-65D — RB-66C — GAM-67 — XB-68 — SM-68

ROCKWELL B-I

U.S. BOMBERS

By

LLOYD S. JONES

D1223400

U.S. BOMBERS

To my wife, Peggy; to Scott, who knows what a contrail is; and to Mark, who soon will.

U.S. BOMBERS

By

LLOYD S. JONES

1974

AERO PUBLISHERS, INC.
329 Aviation Road Fallbrook, Cal. 92028

Library of Congress Cataloging in Publication Data

Jones, Lloyd S   1931-
U. S. bombers.

1. Bombers—History. 2. Ballistic missiles—History. 3. Guided missiles—History. 4. Aeronautics, Military—United States—History. I. Title.
TL685.3.J68   1974   623.74'63'0973   74-81451
ISBN 0-8168-9126-5

Printed and Published in the United States by Aero Publishers, Inc.

TABLE OF CONTENTS

INTRODUCTION

B-29'S BOMB JAPAN! GENERAL DOOLITTLE BOMBS TOKYO FROM CARRIER BASED BOMBERS! B-17'S RAID BERLIN! GENERAL MITCHELL SINKS BATTLESHIP FROM AIRPLANE!

Bombers have been the backbone of an offensive military force for years. Now, with one notable exception, they are stepping aside for the more deadly ballistic missile. This exception is the North American Aviation XB-70 Valkyrie bomber. Although the design of ballistic missiles was foremost immediately following World War II, a parallel development of the more familiar and conventional manned bomber was also underway. Alongside Bomarc missiles, B-47's and B-52's were being built; Atlases and Hustlers were being assembled simultaneously. Some of the technology and theories overlapped, with missile and airplane blending into one unit. This is the case of the XB-70, which is sometimes referred to as a manned missile, having been a direct development of the SM-64 Navaho.

We all know of the exploits of the B-17 Flying Fortress, B-24 Liberator, B-25 Mitchell, and B-29 Superfortress, but few have ever heard of the B-1 Super Cyclops, B-21 Dragon, or the B-33 Super Marauder. Of the aircraft which were assigned "B" designations by the U. S. Army Air Corps or U. S. Air Force, fourteen were no more than "Blueprint Bombers," that is, design studies that became obsolete before production was started, or concepts that were not feasible for the use intended. Some designations were merely proposed engine changes which did not materialize. Othere were just too advanced. Many of the designations were assigned to single prototypes or modifications of familiar production aircraft.

As the Missile Age came into being, some of the new weapons were assigned "B" designations, but these have been redesignated by letters more in keeping with their missions. However, the numerical sequence has been retained as they are considered unmanned bombers. In one instance there is a duplication of numbers assigned. This occurs in the case of the Martin XB-68 supersonic bomber project and the Martin SM-68 Tital missile. Both appear in this book; the XB-68 as a provisional drawing, as the project is classified at this writing.

One other overlap occurs with the Martin B-26 Marauder and the redesignated Douglas A-26 Invader. The Douglas aircraft was reclassified as a light bomber following World War II, and since the Martin type was no longer in service, the Invader became the B-26.

The fact that bombers have had an influence on other fields in aviation is undeniable. A spacious aircraft with a large payload capacity is an ideal framework for a passenger transport. In some cases, bombers became transports, or served as a basis for a new airframe for commercial service. Many foreign airlines are praising the rugged ability of the American bomber in passenger service. Countless private companies and individuals have made war surplus bombers into fast, comfortable personal transports, virtual flying palaces. The experience gained from operating the B-47 and B-52 led to the development of the 707 Jet Stratoliner and KC-135 tanker. The U. S. Coast Guard modified World War II vintage B-17's for air rescue service. Other retired Fortresses became engine test beds for more advanced propulsion systems or vanished in a brilliant flash as the target for a defensive missile.

Although the designation B-1 indicates the first bomber type, it was in fact preceded by many aircraft in the same service category. However, these were assigned more descriptive, though often complicated, designations such as XNBL-1 (Experimental Night Bombardment, Long Range), LB-5 (Light Bombardment), and NBS-1 (Night Bombardment, Short Range). This complex system of identification was replaced by the present method in May, 1924, although some of the more explicit designations are reappearing, such as RB-57D (Reconnaissance Bomber).

With the development of the swing-wing Rockwell B-1A the numbering sequence was begun again. On September 18, 1962, the Defense Department revised the designating system and began each category at -1 again. This book is intended to illustrate the development of the American bomber, step by step, from the Keystone XB-1 biplane of 1928 to the Rockwell B-1A supersonic weapon of the 1980's.

ACKNOWLEDGEMENT

I would like to express my sincerest thanks to these aviation enthusiasts whose assistance and encouragement have brought about this history:

Bude Donato and Harry Gann of the American Aircraft Historical Society; Royal D. Frey, Chief, Reference and Research Division, Air Force Museum; Malcolm H. Holloway, General Dynamics (Convair); Eric Miller, Lockheed California; Harl V. Brackin, Jr., Boeing; Crosby Maynard, Douglas; Kenneth D. Engle, Martin Co.; John Ball, Jr. Defense Marketing Services; Ray Wagner; E. W. Robischon, IAS; and the countless others who have contributed to this project.

PHOTO CREDIT

Air Force Museum: Figs. 1 - 3 - 4 - 7 - 12 - 20 - 71 - 80 - 160 - 162 - 163 - 164.

Lowell Dixon: Figs. 6 - 15 - 43.

Ray Wagner: Figs. 8 - 10 - 11 - 24.

Douglas Aircraft Co., Inc.: Figs. 13 - 16 - 29 - 31 - 53 - 55 - 57 - 60 - 61 - 62 - 73 - 76 - 168 - 169 - 258.

North American Aviation, Inc.: Figs. 17 - 19 - 69 - 72 - 90 - 92 - 93 - 95 - 97 - 98 - 105 - 107 - 175 - 177 - 247 - 249 - 250.

The Boeing Company: Figs. 21 - 23 - 33 - 35 - 36 - 45 - 46 - 47 - 49 - 50 - 108 - 110 - 184 - 185 - 186 - 187 - 195 - 197 - 201 - 203 - 204 - 205 - 207 - 208 - 214 - 220.

The Martin Co.: Figs. 25 - 27 - 99 - 101 - 188 - 190 - 198 - 200 - 221 - 223 - 225 - 236 - 238 - 266 - 268.

Harry Gann (Douglas): Figs. 32 - 54 - 59 - 75 - 165 - 167 - 171 - 255.

Lloyd S. Jones: Figs. 37 - 39 - 40 - 42 - 66 - 68 - 102 - 104 - 111 - 113 - 114 - 116 - 125 - 127 - 128 - 130 - 147 - 149 - 209 - 212 - 215 - 217 - 218 - 230 - 263 - 265 - 273 - 275 - 276.

National Aeronautics and Space Administration: Figs. 63 - 65.

Convair, Division of General Dynamics Corp.: Figs. 77 - 79 - 81 - 82 - 84 - 86 - 88 - 89 - 117 - 119 - 120 - 121 - 123 - 124 - 138 - 140 - 141 - 142 - 143 - 144 - 145 - 146 - 178 - 180 - 181 - 211 - 226 - 228 - 229 - 232 - 234 - 235 - 251 - 253 - 254.

Bob Vier, California Hobby Dist.: Fig. 85.

Gordon Gurnee: Fig. 96.

Lockheed Aircraft Corp.: Figs. 131 - 133 - 150 - 152 - 156 - 158 - 159 - 269 - 272.

U. S. A. F.: Figs. 182 - 257.

Northrop Corp.: Figs. 134 - 136 - 137 - 191 - 193 - 194 - 239 - 241 - 242.

Air Technical Service Command: Figs. 153 - 155.

Pratt & Whitney: Figs. 172 - 174.

Bell Aircraft: Figs. 243 - 245 - 246.

Radioplane Div. Norair: Figs. 259 - 261 - 262.

Jerry Kishpaugh: Fig. 271.

KEYSTONE
XB-1 SUPER CYCLOPS

Fig. 1. XB-1 Note gunners position on rear portion of engine nacelle.

The first plane in the new basic "B" category for bombardment type aircraft was originally designed by the Huff-Daland Company, but delivered to the Army by the newly formed Keystone Company as the XB-1 in 1928.

The two geared Packard 2A-1530 engines used were unacceptable and the bomber was re-engined with two Curtiss V-1570 Conquerors of 600 hp each. With the new engines, the single example of the Super Cyclops was given the designation XB-1B and had a top speed of 120 mph.

Unique among its contemporaries, the XB-1B carried two of its crew of five in gun turrets in the aft portion of the engine nacelles. Each gunner was armed with two Lewis machine guns firing rearward. Another gunner, similarly armed, was located in the nose of the plane. Operational bomb load was 2,508 pounds with a range of 700 miles.

Dimensions of the XB-1 remained the same following conversion to the XB-1B. The single bay wings spanned 85 feet; length of the aircraft was 62 feet, and it stood 19 feet 3 inches high. Empty weight was 9,462 pounds, gross weight 16,500 pounds, and 444 gallons of fuel were carried. Service ceiling was 15,000 feet. Maximum gross weight was 17,039 pounds; wing area 1,604 square feet; landing speed 56 mph.

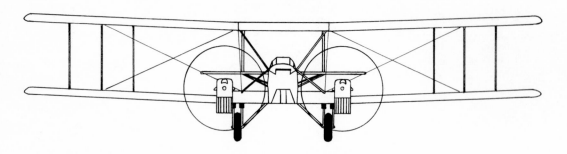

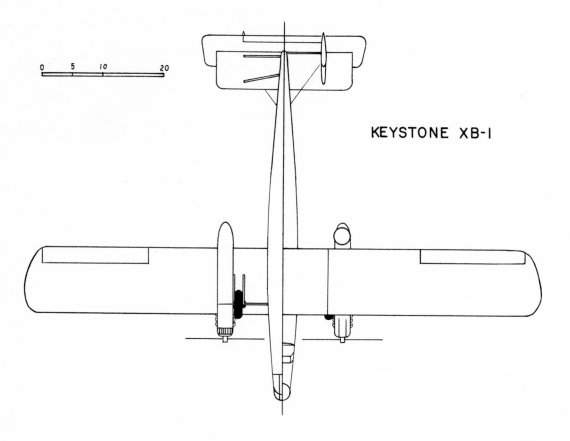

KEYSTONE XB-1

0 5 10 20

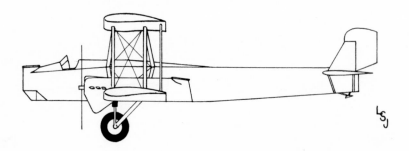

Fig. 2. Keystone XB-1 Super Cyclops.

Fig. 3. Keystone (Huff Daland) XB-1 with two Packard engines. First of the "B" series of bombers.

CURTISS
B-2 CONDOR

Fig. 4. Curtiss XB-2 Condor, serial number A.C. 25-211.

In development at the same time as the Keystone XB-1, the Curtiss XB-2 was quite similar but proved to be the superior aircraft. Like the Keystone design, the XB-2 also mounted dual Lewis guns in turrets located in the rear of the engine nacelles.

A crew of five was carried by this bomber with a performance rating that placed it far above any planes in its class. Testing of the XB-2 began in September, 1927, and though the qualities were superior to competing types, the higher cost of the B-2 resulted in a limited production order of only 12 planes in June, 1928. The first B-2 was delivered in May, 1929.

Production models of the B-2 were powered by two Curtiss Conqueror V-1570-7 engines of 630 hp, providing a top speed of 130 mph and a rate of climb of 850 feet per minute. They could carry 2,500 pounds of bombs for 780 miles, and had a service ceiling of 17,100 feet. Empty, the B-2 weighed 9,039 pounds and grossed 16,516 pounds. The largest of the biplane types in this series, the B-2 had a wingspan of 90 feet, but a length of only 47 feet 6 inches. Height was 16 feet 3 inches; wing area was 1,499 square feet. Cruising speed, 114 mph; landing speed, 53 mph; absolute ceiling, 19,400 feet; fuel capacity, 444 gallons.

In view of the excellent performance of the Condor, it is interesting to note the biplane tail assembly used. Production B-2's were the first aircraft of the type to incorporate tail wheels instead of the skid which assisted in braking, but was also responsible for structural failures.

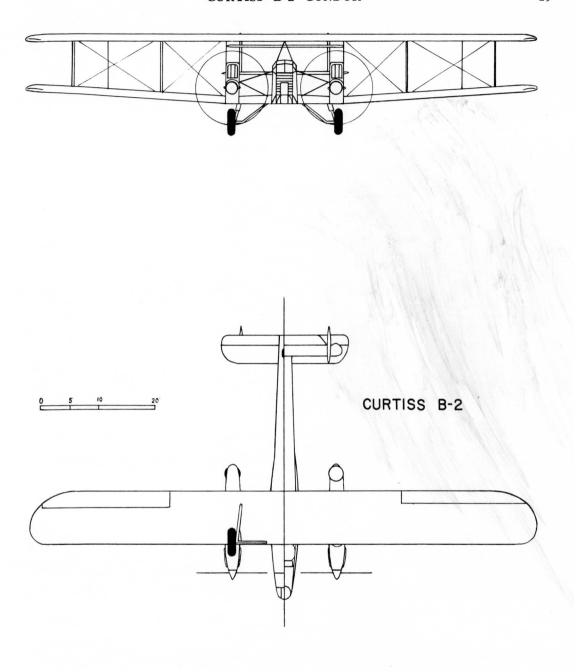

CURTISS B-2

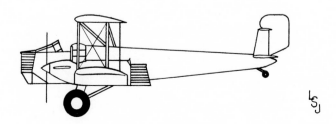

Fig. 5. Curtiss B-2 Condor.

Fig. 6. One of the twelve production B-2's. Note smaller radiators on engines.

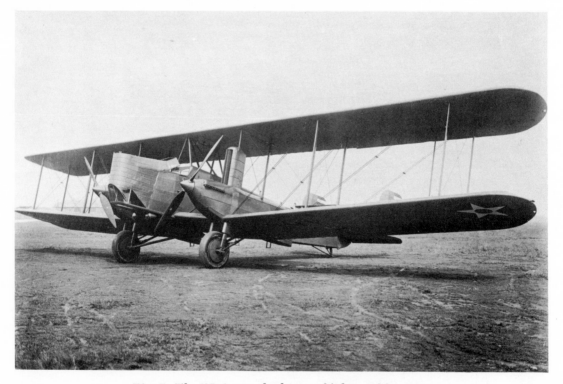

Fig. 7. The XB-2 was the largest biplane of its type.

KEYSTONE
B-3A, B-4A, B-5A, & B-6A PANTHER

Fig. 8. The Keystone B-3A was a conversion of the LB-10A.

The Keystone Panther series of bombers began as the LB-10A, an improvement on the basic Keystone bomber design. Structurally, all the Panthers were basically the same, the difference being in the engine changes. The B-3A was actually the production version of the LB-10A and was powered by two 525 hp Pratt & Whitney R-1690-3 Hornet radial air-cooled engines. These gave a top speed to 114 mph and rate of climb of 650 feet per minute. Service ceiling of the B-3A was 12,700 feet, with a range of 860 miles. Empty and gross weights were 7,705 pounds and 12,952 pounds. Thirty-six B-3A's were delivered to the Army, three of these becoming Y1B-6's.

Five Y1B-4's, powered by Pratt & Whitney R-1860-7 Hornet B's of 575 hp, were converted from the similar LB-13

type. Production B-4A's numbered 25 and the more powerful engines increased the top speed to 121 mph and the service ceiling to 14,000 feet. Empty weight was raised to 7,951 pounds while the gross was 13,209 pounds, and the range was 855 miles.

Like the previous planes in this series, the Y1B-5 was a conversion; its progenitor being the former LB-14. This variation was supplied with two Wright R-1750-3 Cyclone 9 engines rated at 525 hp and giving a top speed of 111 mph. Empty, the B-5A weighed 7,705 pounds and grossed 12,925 pounds. Rate of climb was reduced to 540 feet per minute, and service ceiling to 10,600 feet. Range of the B-5A was 815 miles. Following the initial three Y1B-5's were 27 production B-5A's.

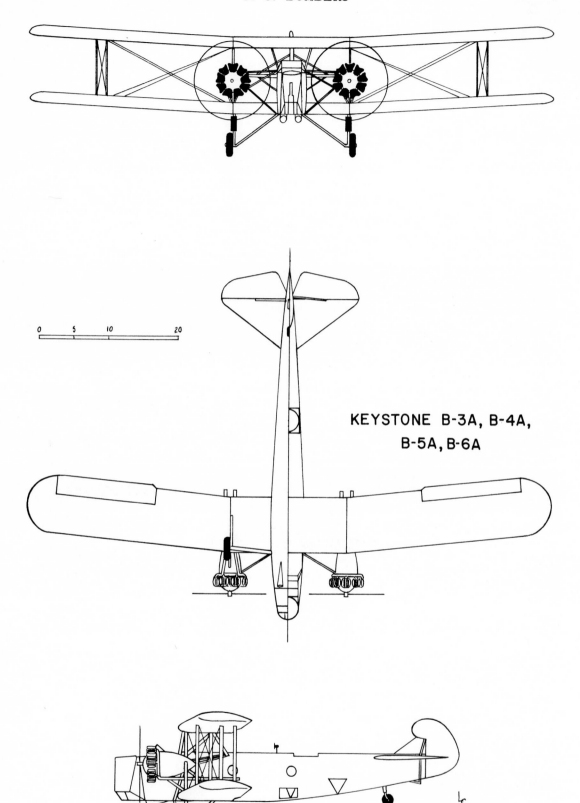

KEYSTONE B-3A, B-4A,
B-5A, B-6A

Fig. 9. Keystone B-3A, B-4A, B-5A, B-6A Panther.

Heralding the end of the biplane generation of heavy bombardment type airplanes was the Keystone B-6A. Two LB-13's and three B-3A's were re-engined with the 575 hp Wright R-1820-1 Cyclone 9 engines. These five planes were then designated Y1B-6, and following testing, a production order was placed for 39 B-6A's. This version was the heaviest of the Panther series, grossing 13,374 pounds. Service ceiling was 14,100 feet and range was 825 miles. Rate of climb was improved to 690 feet per minute.

The Keystone B-3, B-4, B-5, B-6 Panther series had a span of 74 feet 9 inches, wing area of 1,145 square feet, length of 48 feet 10 inches, and a height of 17 feet 2 inches. A crew of 5 was carried. Fuel capacity was 535 gallons; landing speed, 57 mph. Absolute ceiling was 16,500 feet (B-6A). The total number procured, either converted or through production, was 140. All versions were armed with three .30 cal. Browning machine guns.

Fig. 10. Keystone B-4A Panther.

Fig. 11. The B-5A was powered by two Cyclones.

Fig. 12. The B-6A version of the Panther was the last American biplane bomber.

DOUGLAS
Y1B-7

Fig. 13. Prototype Douglas XB-7, serial number 30-228.

The Douglas B-7 was a transitional product of the new theories of a new era. Although a monoplane design, it appeared to be reluctant to part with the strength-giving struts that typified the age of the biplane. In fact, it looked like a biplane with one wing missing.

The Y1B-7 was a development of the Douglas 0-35 observation plane. The XB-7 was the second XO-35 airframe, modified into a fast day bomber. The fuselage was all metal, corrugated for strength. The fabric covered wings were of all metal frame construction and all control surfaces were entirely of metal. This same construction was used on the seven Y1B-7's that followed, except that the fuselages on the latter were not corrugated.

The landing gear retracted hydraulically into the engine nacelle behind the two Curtiss V-1570-27 Conqueror engines which delivered 675 hp each. The nacelles themselves were suspended from struts and hung below the high gull wing. The Y1B-7 carried a crew of four and 1,200 pounds of bombs for 411 miles. Top speed was 182 mph and rate of climb was 1,325 feet per minute to a service ceiling of 20,400 feet. Absolute ceiling was 21,800 feet; cruising speed, 158 mph; landing speed 78 mph; maximum range, 632 miles. The Douglas Y1B-7 weighed 7,519 pounds empty with a gross of 9,953 pounds. Armament consisted of two .30 cal. Browning machine guns; one in the nose, and the other in a turret aft of the wing.

The Y1B-7's wing had a span of 65 feet 3 inches and an area of 621 square feet, small in comparison with the earlier biplanes. Length was 46 feet 6 inches, and height was 12 feet 1 inch.

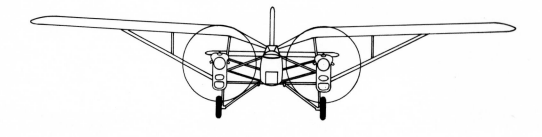

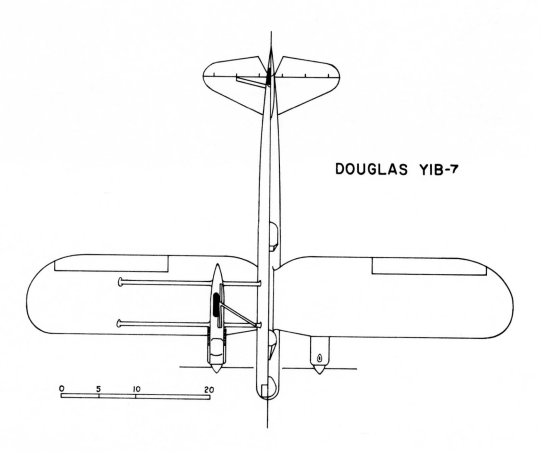

DOUGLAS Y1B-7

0   5   10   20

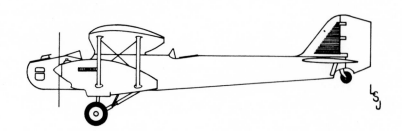

Fig. 14. Douglas Y1B-7

Fig. 15. Seven Y1B-7's were delivered to the Air Corps.

Fig. 16. A Y1B-7 of the 31st Bombardment Squadron, Hamilton Field.

FOKKER
XB-8

Fig. 17. The XB-8 was converted from the 2nd XO-27.

With the appearance of the Fokker XB-8, the last vestiges of the biplane age were gone from bomber design. An airplane of such clean lines had never before worn the colors of a U. S. Army bomber. A true cantilever design, there were no drag-producing struts or wailing rigging to reduce the efficiency of the XB-8. Like the Douglas B-7, this plane also was modified from an observation design; in this case, the Fokker 0-27.

Ordered in February, 1929, with the XB-7, the sole example of the Fokker XB-8 was ready for testing in 1930. The plywood wing was shoulder mounted on the fabric covered, metal tube fuselage. The traditional nose gunner position was equipped with a sliding streamlined cover, and the fuselage side, forward of the wing, was strengthened by a corrugated panel extending to the nose.

Mounted almost entirely within the wing were two Curtiss Conqueror V-1520--23 600 hp engines yielding a speed of 160 mph. The retractable landing gear was pulled into large wells located in the rear portion of the engine fairings. But in spite of its sleek appearance, the performance of the XB-8 did not merit a production order and it was ultimately restored to the 0-27 configuration.

Empty weight of the XB-8 was 6,861 pounds and gross weight, including 209½ gallons of fuel, was 10,545 pounds. The plywood covered, internally braced wing had an area of 619 square feet and a span of 64 feet. Overall length and height were 47 feet and 11 feet 6 inches.

Shortly after the appearance of the XB-8, the Fokker Company was reorganized as the General Aviation Manufacturing Corp. and this aircraft is sometimes referred to as the General XB-8.

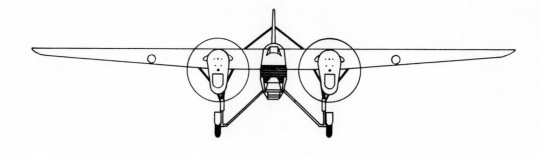

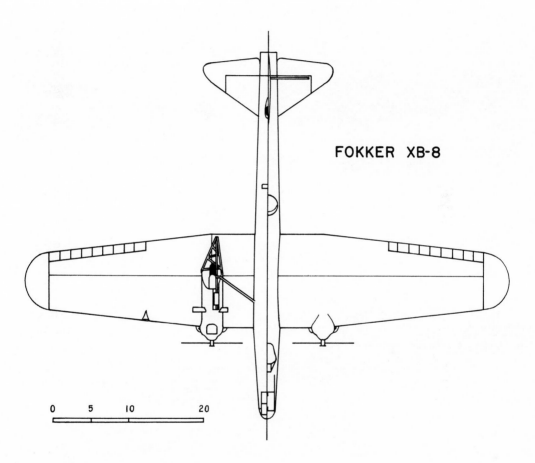

FOKKER XB-8

0   5   10   20

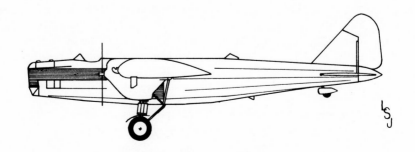

Fig. 18. Fokker XB-8.

Fig. 19. The XB-8 during a landing gear retraction test.

Fig. 20. The Fokker XO-27 observation plane.

BOEING
Y1B-9A

Fig. 21. Boeing Model 215 or XB-901. Serial number 32-301.

In 1930, the Boeing Aircraft Co. introduced a new aerodynamic concept to the commercial airways in the form of a low wing, single engine monoplane constructed entirely of metal. Known as the Model 200 Monomail, this design was so successful Boeing enlarged upon it and built a twin engine, high speed bomber, designating it XB-901, or Model 215.

On April 29, 1931, the XB-901 took off on its first flight powered by two 575 hp Pratt & Whitney R-1860-13 Hornet B engines which gave it a speed capability of 163 mph. Five months later, the Army ordered six units for service evaluation, to be called B-9, the designation YB-9 being assigned to the XB-901 prototype. The second airframe was then modified to use Curtiss V-1570-29 Conqueror 600

hp inline engines in slim, bullet-like nacelles, and was labled Y1B-9. With these engines, it reached 173 mph with a service ceiling of 19,200 feet. The five remaining aircraft were designated Y1B-9A and powered by Pratt & Whitney Y1G1R-1860B supercharged Hornets of 600 hp. These engines had been tested on the XB-901 following Army procurement. Although the five Y1B-9A's were similar externally to the prototypes, they featured several structural modifications and improvements which led to a top speed of 188 mph and a service ceiling of 20,150 feet. The speed of the Y1B-9A was such that the pursuit planes of the day could only pursue it. With a crew of four, the Y1B-9A was armed with a .30 cal. machine gun in the nose and dorsal turrets, and

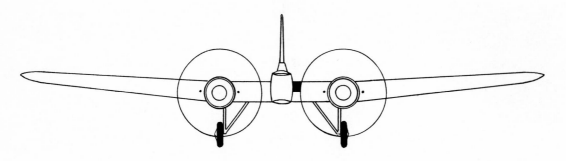

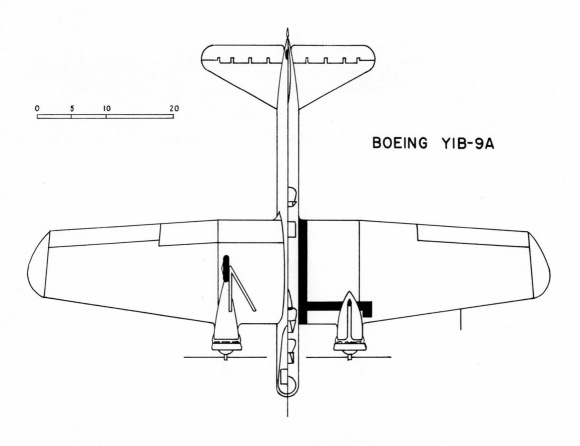

BOEING YIB-9A

0   5   10   20

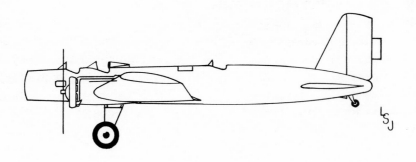

Fig. 22. Boeing Y1B-9A.

Fig. 23. Boeing's Y1B-9A carried a crew of four in the long fuselage.

could carry 2,200 pounds of bombs for 540 miles. Absolute range with a lighter load was 990 miles. The Y1B-9A weighed 8,941 pounds and grossed 13,932 pounds, (1,269 pounds more than the gross weight of the XB-901.) The wingspan was 76 feet 10 inches; length, 52 feet; and height, 12 feet. Wing area was 954 square feet, cruising speed 165 mph, landing speed 65 mph, rate of climb 900 feet per minute, absolute ceiling 22,500 feet, and fuel capacity 526 gallons.

Fig. 24. The Y1B-9 (32-302) with 600 hp Conqueror engines.

MARTIN
B-10B, B-12A, XB-13, & XB-14

Fig. 25. The B-10 was the first monoplane bomber to reach full production.

The first of the new generation of bombers to actually achieve full production was the Martin B-10, B-12 series, including the unbuilt XB-13 and the single XB-14.

Initially introduced in mid 1932 as the XB-907, or Martin Model 123, the prototype differed primarily from the production B-10's in having three open cockpits and speedring type cowlings on the two Wright SR-1820-E Cyclones. In this configuration, a top speed of 197 mph was obtained. Following preliminary testing, it was decided to replace the forward turret with a power-operated dome, increase the span 8 feet 5 inches, and install more powerful Wright R-1820-19's of 675 hp with redesigned cowlings. Four months after the XB-907 was first flown, it reappeared with these changes. Designated by Martin XB-907A, it was subsequently tagged XB-10 by the Army and given the serial number 33-139. The improvements stepped up the top speed to 207 mph.

Results of the prototype tests were so outstanding, the Army ordered 15 copies in January, 1933, for service evaluation. Fourteen to be YB-10's (later to become B-10M) with R-1820-25 engines of 675 hp, and one YB-10A with turbo supercharged R-1820-31 engines which produced a speed of 236 mph and a rate of climb in excess of 1,400 feet per minute. At the same time, seven additional planes were ordered with the 775 hp Pratt & Whitney R-1690-11 Hornet A's designated YB-12 and twenty-five more YB-12A's with a larger fuel capacity for longer range.

All the new models featured enclosed cockpits for the crew of four. The mechanically retracting landing gear was retained.

One further type was tested with Pratt & Whitney R-1830-9 Twin Wasps of 800 hp and identified as XB-14 (U.S.A.A.F. serial 33-162). It was proposed to power an additional twelve planes with Pratt & Whitney R-1860-17 Hornet B's of 575 hp. These were to become B-13's; however,

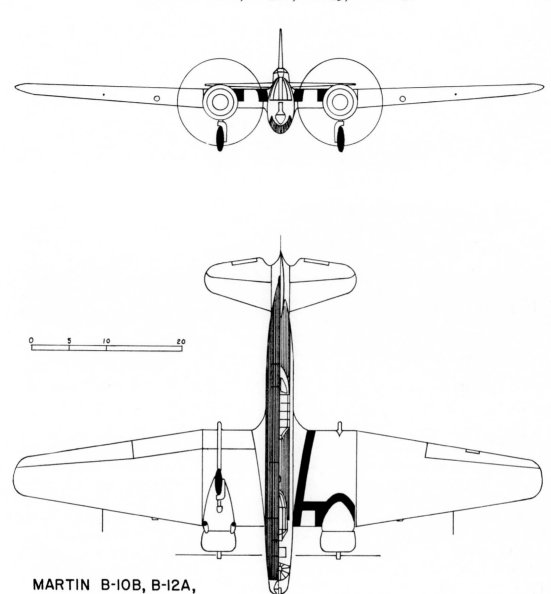

MARTIN B-10B, B-12A,
XB-13, XB-14

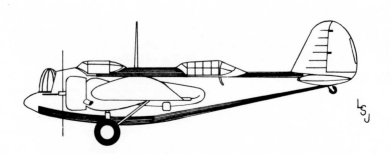

Fig. 26. Martin B-10B, B-12A, XB-13, XB-14.

Fig. 27. Martin B-10B.

no B-13 aircraft were built.

The B-10B was the model of which most were produced, and was powered by Wright R-1820-33 Cyclones. The three guns carried, located in the nose turret, floor, and rear canopy, were .30 cal. Brownings. A maximum bomb load, weighing 2,260 pounds, could be transported 1,240 miles.

Dimensions of the B-10, B-12 series were as follows: span, 70 feet 6 inches; length, 44 feet 8 11/16 inches; height, 15 feet 5 inches; wing area, 678 square feet. B-10B weighed 9,681 pounds empty, and grossed 14,600 pounds. The cruising

speed was 193 mph, with a landing speed of 65 mph.

The performance and durability of the design was proven when, on July 19, 1934, ten planes left on a 7,360 mile round trip between Washington, D. C., and Fairbanks, Alaska. One of the planes was ditched in Cook Inlet in Alaska, but owing to the watertight wings and stabilizers, the plane was recovered and made the return trip.

A total of 121 B-10's, 32 B-12's, and one XB-14 were ordered by the Army Air Corps; a design that was so successful, it won for Glenn L. Martin the Collier Trophy for 1932.

Fig. 28. The B-12A was structurally similar to the B-10 but was powered by two Pratt & Whitney engines.

DOUGLAS
YB-11

Fig. 29. As the YOA-5, the YB-11 became the forerunner of the Air Rescue craft used today by the Air Force.

The YB-11 was the only bomber designed for the Air Corps for the dual role of land and sea operation. Shortly after Douglas had developed the XP3D-1, a large twin engine seaplane, for the U. S. Navy as a patrol bomber, the Army ordered a scaled down version to be built as an amphibian.

Powered by two Wright R-1820-45 Cyclones rated at 930 hp, the YB-11 was to have a crew of five and carry three .30 cal. machine guns. One gun was located in the plexiglas nose turret, and one each in waist positions which were covered by sliding hatches when not in use. The forward part of the wing was of corrugated aluminum with fabric covering from the rear spar back. The fuselage was all metal and the landing gear retracted into depressed wells on the sides.

Before completion, the design was reclassified as an observation type and given the designation YO-44. However, the finished product was delivered with the Air Corps serial number 33-17 as the YOA-5 amphibian. It bore this identification throughout its life as one of the fore-runners of the Air Rescue planes of today.

The YB-11, or YOA-5, had a top speed of 169 mph and a gross weight of 20,000 pounds. The shoulder-mounted wing spread to 89 feet 9 inches, and the overall length was 69 feet 9 inches. Height was approximately 22 feet.

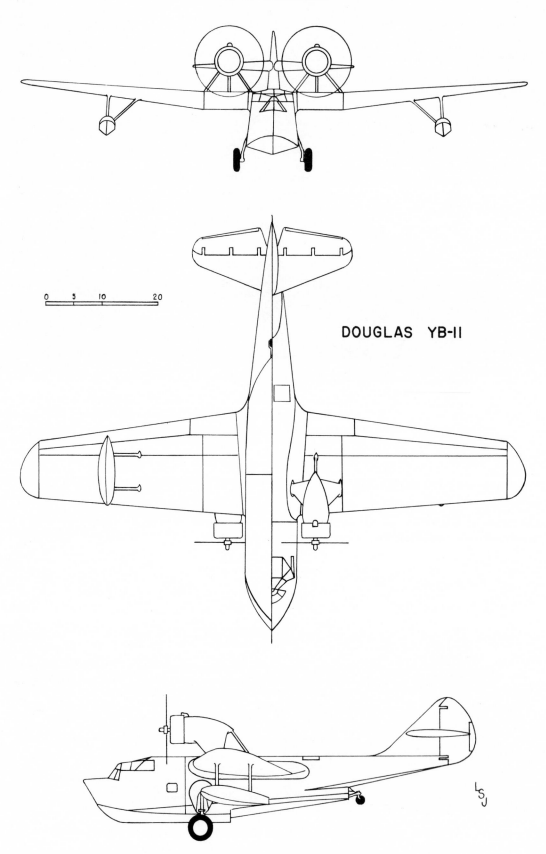

0   5   10   20

DOUGLAS YB-11

Fig. 30. Douglas YB-11

Fig. 31. Douglas YB-11 was the only amphibian bomber to be ordered by the Air Corps.

Fig. 32. The Douglas XP3D-1 was quite similar in appearance to the YB-11.

BOEING
XB-15

Fig. 33. Boeing Model 294, U. S. Air Corps XB-15. This plane later became the XC-105.

In March, 1938, the Army Air Corps took delivery on by far the most advanced and impressive aircraft to fit the bomber concept. An all metal giant with a span of 149 feet and a length of 87 feet 7 inches, the new Boeing XB-15 required dual wheels to support its maximum weight of 70,706 pounds.

Engineering work on the large four engine, long range bomber began in January, 1934. On June 29, 1935, the proposal was given the designation XB-15 and the A.A.F. serial number 35-277. Four 14 cylinder Pratt & Whitney R-1830-11 engines were selected to give a total of 3,400 hp. Although the XB-15 was the first four engine bomber ordered by the Air

Corps, it did not fly until after the smaller B-17. Flight testing began on August 15, 1937, and the results showed a speed of 197 mph, a service ceiling of 18,850 feet, and a range of 5,130 miles.

The four Twin Wasp engines did not deliver enough power to show a spectacular performance so the XB-15 was placed in a cargo carrying category and, with a large door cut into the fuselage side, spent the remainder of its life as the XC-105. (This was actually the third designation for the plane. For a short time during construction, it was classed in a new group of experimental long range bombers as the XBLR-1.)

Performing as a bomber, the XB-15

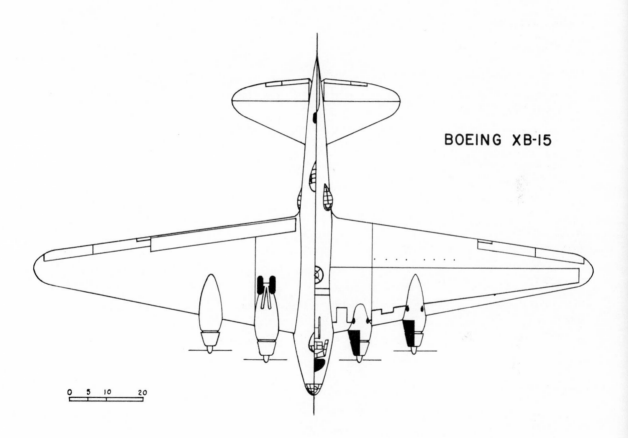

BOEING XB-15

0 5 10   20

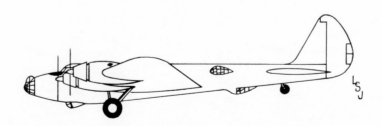

Fig. 34. Boeing XB-15.

Fig. 35. To support its weight of 70,700 pounds, the XB-15 used dual main wheels.

was not outstanding, but it had many new features that paved the way for those that followed. The 110 volt electrical system was the first in any airplane. Complete comfort-conditioned living and sleeping quarters, including a kitchenette and lavatory, were provided for the crew of ten. The thick wings held a passageway to each of the engines for inflight servicing, and a special station was furnished in the cockpit for a flight engineer.

As the largest aircraft yet built in the United States, the XB-15 had a bomb capacity of 2,511 pounds which it could carry for 3,500 miles. It was also the most heavily armed bomber to appear,

being defended by three .30 and three .50 cal. guns placed in six turrets with a total of 7,200 rounds of ammunition. It had a wing span of 149 feet, wing area of 2,781 square feet, length of 87 feet 7 inches, and height of 19 feet 5 inches. It weighed 37,700 pounds empty and grossed 65,068 pounds, with a fuel capacity of 4,190 gallons. Cruising speed was 171 mph, landing speed 70 mph. It had a rate of climb of 700 feet per minute, and an absolute ceiling of 20,900 feet.

As a transport, the XC-105 set several payload records, and in 1945, after more than eight years of flying, the first American "heavy" bomber was disassembled.

Fig. 36. When the XB-15 first flew, it was the largest plane in the world.

MARTIN
XB-16

Fig. 37. This XB-16 design featured retractable fuselage gun turrets.

Late in 1934, the Martin Company laid down a proposal for a fast, long range, heavy bomber, the Martin Model 145-A, and received the Air Corps designation XB-16. Though conforming to the new concept of large bombardment types and utilizing four engines, the XB-16 design deviated from the bulky, air cooled radials now receiving wide acceptance. Four 1,000 hp Allison V-1710 liquid cooled engines were buried entirely in the wings driving 12 foot 3 inch propellers via extension shafts. The inboard nacelles were enlarged to accommodate the dual five foot tires of the landing gear. Estimated top speed, with supercharging, at 20,000 feet was 237 mph. Service ceiling was placed at 22,500 feet with a rate of climb of 740 feet per minute. A landing speed of 60 mph was anticipated by the use of Fowler type flaps of 360 square feet which spanned 80 feet.

Defensive armament was to be carried in plexiglas nose and tail enclosures and retractable dorsal and ventral turrets. A bomb load of 12,180 pounds was to be transported 3,200 miles, and flight endurance with 4,238 gallons of fuel was 42 hours. A crew of ten was to have operated the aircraft.

Span, 140 feet; length, 84 feet; height, 19 feet 7 inches; wing area, 2,600 square feet; empty weight, 31,957 pounds; gross weight, 65,000 pounds; useful load, 33,043 pounds; normal bomb load, 2,500 pounds; cruising speed, 120 mph; normal range, 5,040 miles; maximum range (no bombs), 6,200 miles.

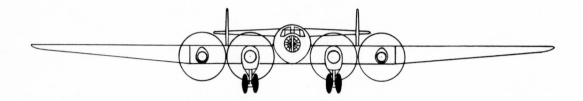

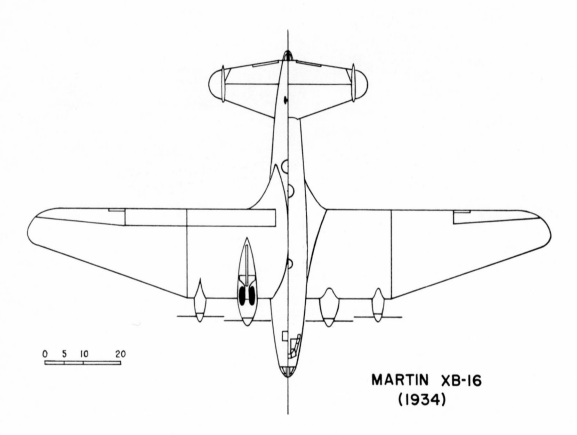

MARTIN XB-16
(1934)

0   5   10   20

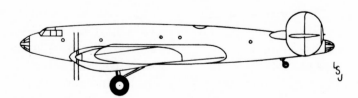

Fig. 38. Martin XB-16 (1934).

Fig. 39. This photo shows a model of the Martin design 145-A, XB-16 proposal.

MARTIN
XB-16 (FINAL DESIGN)

Fig. 40. Model showing final design development of Martin XB-16 program.

Continued development of the original XB-16 design in 1935 led to a grotesque giant featuring a huge 4,256 square foot wing to which two thin tail booms were attached. An unusual podded, nacelle type fuselage housing the payload and crew of ten was suspended beneath the wing. Six buried Allison V-1710-3 engines were located in a unique four tractor, two pusher arrangement driving their propellers through extension shafts. Maximum speed anticipated was 256 mph, cruising at 140 mph, with a range of 3,300 miles. Bomb load was 2,500 pounds. Fuel tanks were to have a 7,435 gallon capacity.

It is interesting to note the first ap-

pearance of the tricycle type landing gear on this projected design. The large diameter main tires were partially exposed when the gear retracted into the wing. Estimated landing speed was 77 mph.

Wing span of this XB-16 configuration was to be 173 feet, the twin rudders extending to 114 feet 10 inches behind the nose. An empty weight of 50,660 pounds was determined with the gross being 104,880 pounds.

Although the engineering design was purchased by the A.A.F., no models of the Martin XB-16 were built and the project was cancelled.

MARTIN XB-16 (Final Design)   43

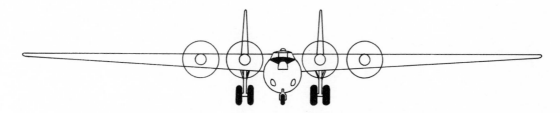

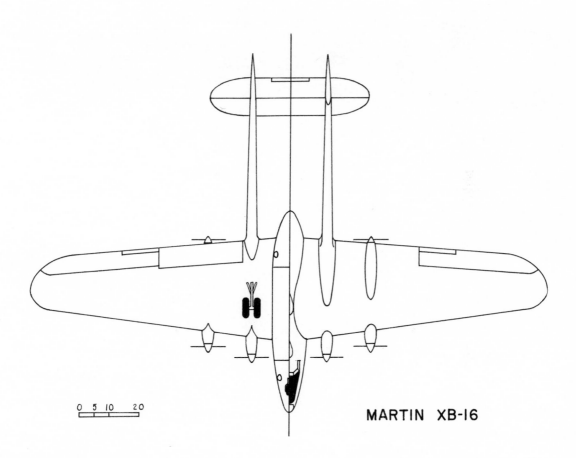

0 5 10   20

MARTIN XB-16

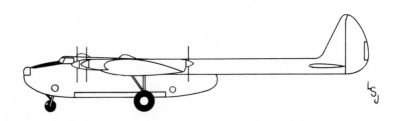

Fig. 41. Martin XB-16.

Fig. 42. Note the unusual positioning of the six buried Allison engines.

BOEING
YB-17 FLYING FORTRESS

Fig. 43. A YB-17 in service with the U. S. Air Corps.

On August 16, 1934, Boeing began construction of a four engine heavy bomber with which it hoped to win a twin engine competition for the U.S.A.A.F.'s new standard bearer. Financed by the company itself, the Boeing Model 299 lifted into the air on July 28, 1935, and led the way for one of the world's most famous series of airplanes.

The new design appeared as a scaled down version of the, as yet unfinished, XB-15, since much of the latter's engineering principles had been applied to the smaller craft. Performance of the 299 immediately overshadowed that of its two engined competitors. The four Pratt & Whitney R-1690-E Hornets, each offering 750 hp, provided a top speed of 250 mph and a service ceiling of 25,000 feet. Among the new features incorporated into the Model 299 were control locks designed to keep the wind from buffeting the large moveable surfaces while on the ground. On October 30, 1935, during Air Corps tests, this innovation was tragically over-

looked and, after taking off with the controls locked, the 299 fell to its destruction.

But Boeing's gamble paid off when on January 17, 1936, thirteen planes were ordered. As the YB-17, the first Flying Fortress (A.F. serial number 36-149), was accepted in January, 1937. Power was supplied by Wright R-1820-39 Cyclones of 930 hp, and a top speed of 256 mph was achieved. Service ceiling was 30,600 feet. The maximum range was 3,320 miles. Five and a quarter tons of bombs could be carried 1,377 miles. The six crewmen were armed with five .30 or .50 cal. guns.

The YB-17 had an empty weight of 24,468 pounds and a gross of 34,873 pounds. The 103 foot 9 inch wing had an area of 1,420 square feet and remained basically unchanged in the subsequent models. One YB-17 was fitted with Wright R-1850-21 supercharged engines giving 1,000 hp on take-off and a speed of 295 mph at 25,000 feet. This was the sole YB-17A (serial number 37-369), and was

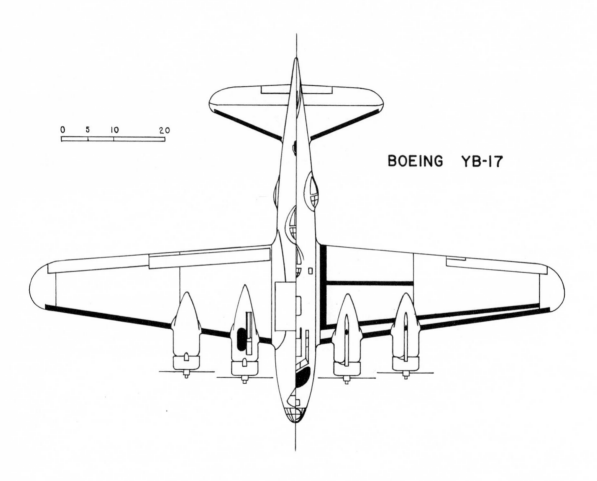

0   5   10   20

BOEING YB-17

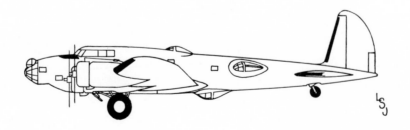

Fig. 44. Boeing YB-17 Flying Fortress.

Fig. 45. This view of a YB-17 shows four of the fuselage gun blisters, each holding one machine gun.

distinguished by the removal of the fairings over the engine nacelles.

The Fortress design was subjected to many modifications in the never ending quest for improved performance. The original 68 foot 4 inch length of the YB-17 differed on some of the later models. The basic changes in the B-17B are as follows: removal of nose blister and bombardier's indentation, length reduced to 67 feet 11 inches, R-1820-51 engines, empty weight of 27,650 pounds, gross 37,810 pounds, fuel capacity 1,700 gallons, top speed of 291 mph, cruising speed 231 mph, service ceiling 36,000 feet, 8,000 pounds of bombs, armament of one .30 cal. and six .50 cal. guns. Thirty-nine B-17B's were built.

Thirty-eight B-17C's, followed by forty-two B-17D's, carried two more .50 cal. guns and had the more powerful 1,200 hp Wright R-1820-65's giving a top speed of 323 mph and a cruise of 250 mph with a 3,400 mile range. Service ceiling was increased to 37,000 feet. The "D"'s had self-sealing fuel tanks.

Fig. 46. One of the thirteen Y1B-17's, later called YB-17.

BOEING
B-17G FLYING FORTRESS

Fig. 47. One of 235 B-17G-45's built by Boeing at Seattle.

In September of 1941, a new Fortress appeared with an extensively modified empennage. Gone was the pert fin and rudder riding precariously behind the stabilizer. Instead, a broad yet graceful dorsal fin rose from amidhsips and enveloped a deadly stinger of twin .50 cal. machine guns. A remote-controlled belly turret held two more. 50's. This was the B-17E, of which 112 were built. Four hundred more followed but with a manned Sperry ball turret replacing the remote system. The B-17E was lengthened to 73 feet 10 inches to accomodate the new defensive tail position. Top speed was 317 mph, cruising at over 200 mph with 4,000 pounds of bombs.

Production of the similar B-17F was undertaken by Douglas and Vega, a subsidiary of the Lockheed Aircraft Corp., as well as the parent Boeing Company. Though the improved 1,200 hp Wright R-1820-97 engines were used on the new models, the increased weight and drag was taking its toll in speed. The B-17F, though now armed with eleven .50 cal. guns, could only reach 299 mph, but landing speed was up to 90 mph! Service ceiling was 37,500 feet and range 2,880 miles. It took twenty-five and a half minutes to climb to 20,000 feet. Three thousand, four hundred B-17F's were produced by the three companies.

By September, 1943, the Flying Fortress showed its final shape. During firepower tests on the XB-40, a modified B-17F, the advantage of a chin turret was clearly proven and a new series, labeled B-17G, sported this nasal appendage. The Bendix turret held two .50 cal. guns and this model had a total of twelve of these weapons with 6,380 rounds of ammunition. In all, there were 8,680 B-17G's built by Boeing, Vega, and Douglas to make this the largest production variation. Following the first Model 299, the Air Corps purchased 12,725 B-17 type aircraft.

B-17G specifications included a span

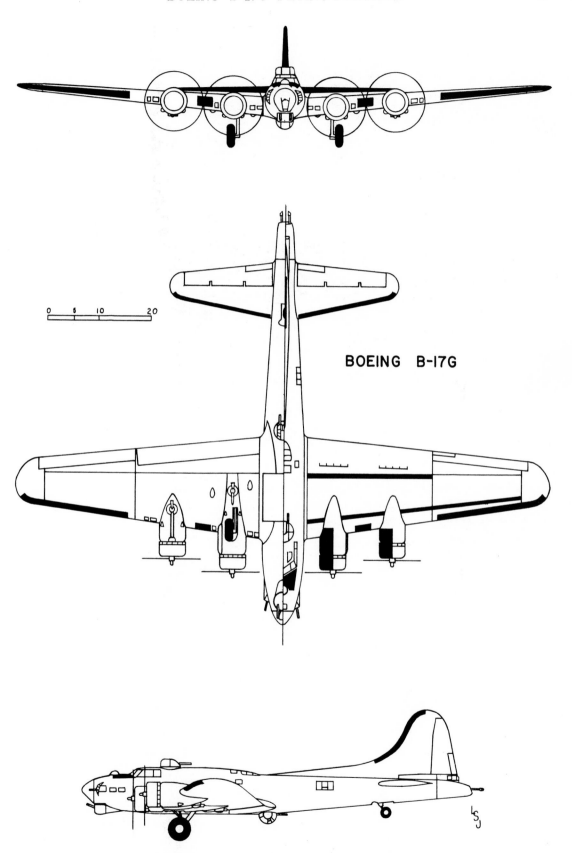

BOEING B-17G

Fig. 48. Boeing B-17G Flying Fortress.

Fig. 49. A Douglas built B-17G-30 from Long Beach, California. Lockheed also manufactured Flying Fortresses for the Air Corps.

of 103 feet 9 inches, length of 74 feet 4 inches, and a height of 19 feet 1 inch. The four supercharged Wright R-1820-97 Cyclones delivered 1,200 hp and gave a top speed of 287 mph, cruising at 182 mph. Service ceiling was 35,600 feet, with a range of 3,400 miles. Empty and gross weights were 36,135 pounds and 55,000 pounds. Maximum fuel load was 3,630 gallons.

Cargo conversions of the B-17 were known as C-108.

Fig. 50. The B-17G introduced new fire power in the form of the Bendix chin turret and a new tail stinger.

DOUGLAS
B-18A AND XB-22 BOLO

Fig. 51. A B-18A in service with the 99th Bombardment Squadron. Note Buffalo insignia below dorsal turret.

The Douglas Aircraft Company entered the 1936 Air Corps bomber competition with a twin engine airplane which showed more than a slight similarity to their new commercial DC-3 airliner. Known as the Douglas Model DB-1, the prototype for the B-18 had a short pug nose and a deep belly which could hold up to 4,400 pounds of bombs. Winning the competition, Douglas received an order for one hundred seventy-seven B-18's to be powered by 930 hp Wright R-1820-45 Cyclones. With a cruising speed of 167 mph and a rate of climb of 1,355 feet per minute, the Bolo had a range of 1,200 miles with its full bomb load. Top speed was 217 mph and the service ceiling was 24,200 feet.

The cramped bombardier's position beneath the nose turret led to a complete redesign of the forward fuselage, placing the bombardier in front and above the nose gun position. This change was made on the one hundred thirty-fourth Bolo which became the first of a total of two hundred seventeen B-18A's. Wright R-1820-53 engines increased the horsepower to 1,000, but a gross weight of 22,123 pounds

---993 pounds more than the B-18 --- reduced the top speed to 215 mph.

The B-18A Bolo was built with watertight outer wing panels and had hydraulically retractable landing gear and flaps. The forward gun position held one .30 cal. machine gun, and a retracting turret just forward of the fin was similarly armed. A third gun was fired through a removeable hatch in the lower fuselage behind the bomb bay.

The B-18 wingspan was 89 feet 6 inches, with an area of 959 square feet. The fuselage length of 56 feet 8 inches was increased to 57 feet 10 inches with the addition of the "shark" nose of the B-18A. The B-18A landed at 68 mph. Fuel capacity could be increased from the normal 802 gallons to 1,170 gallons for a maximum distance of 2,225 miles. Service ceiling of the "A" was 23,900 feet.

The B-18B's were radar-equipped, anti-submarine conversions of one hundred twenty-two B-18A's. The plexiglas bombardier's snout was replaced by a bulbous plastic radome. Some models

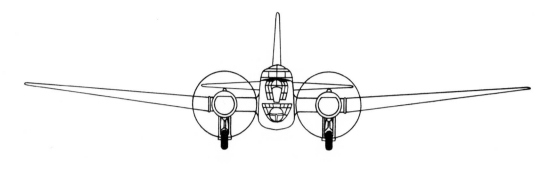

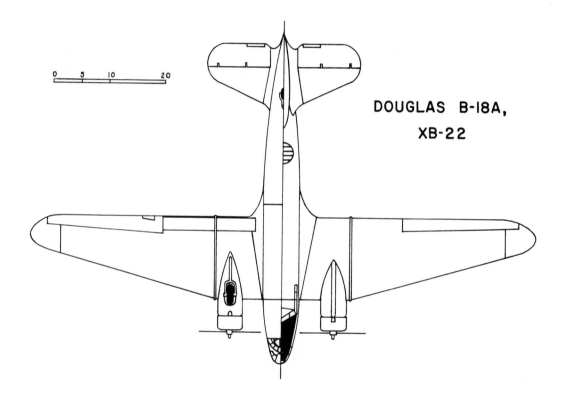

DOUGLAS B-18A,
XB-22

0   5   10   20

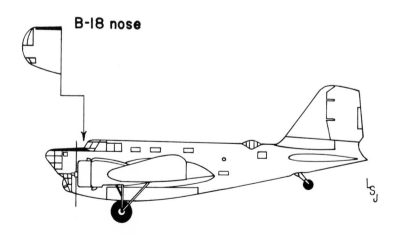

B-18 nose

Fig. 52. Douglas B-18A, XB-22.

Fig. 53. The first 133 B-18's had a smooth nose incorporating a gun turret above the bombardier.

were fitted with tail boom extensions to house additional detection equipment.

The XB-22 was a proposed B-18 airframe with 1,600 hp R-2600-2 Cyclones by Wright. However, the project was dropped in favor of newer models and the XB-22 designation was cancelled.

Fig. 54. This view of a B-18A clearly shows it's decendency from the famed DC-3 commercial airliner. Note lower gunners hatch in aft part of the fuselage.

Fig. 55. A B-18A showing the distinctive "shark nose".

Fig. 56. A pug nosed B-18 from the 72nd Bombardment Squadron.

DOUGLAS
XB-19

Fig. 57. Flight testing of the XB-19 was done with the guns armed and manned following the attack on Pearl Harbor.

On the afternoon of June 27, 1941, a new type of bomber was airborne for the first time. Although not radical in appearance, its size dwarfed all other airplanes. Designated by the Army Air Corps as the XB-19, it was the culmination of seven years of engineering challenges, some so great that the manufacturer had actually requested to be relieved of the project.

Conceived in 1935 as the XBLR-2, the aircraft was given the nineteenth "B" designation and the serial number 38-471 in March, 1938. The largest wing yet built spanned 212 feet; and, like the earlier XB-15, had two sets of ailerons, each pair extending over 45 feet. Following considerable testing on smaller aircraft, its tricycle landing gear became the first used on a bomber. The eight foot main tire retracted almost flush into the lower surface of the wing.

When the XB-19 was delivered to the Air Corps in November of 1941, it was powered by four 2,000 hp Wright R-3350-5 eighteen cylinder Cyclones. Its top speed of 224 mph was not great but the XB-19's defensive armament was tremendous. The nose and top forward power turrets each carried one 37 mm cannon and a .30 cal. machine gun. Single .50 cal. machine guns were located in the powered rear dome, two waist positions, a belly fairing, and the tail. Two more .30's were on each side of the bombardier and in the sides on the empennage for a total of twelve guns with 4,700 rounds of ammunition. Due to the outbreak of World War II, the flight testing of the XB-19 was done with the guns armed.

Propelling a plane with an empty weight of 84,431 pounds and a gross of 140,000 pounds, the performance by the Wright radials was limited. In 1943, four

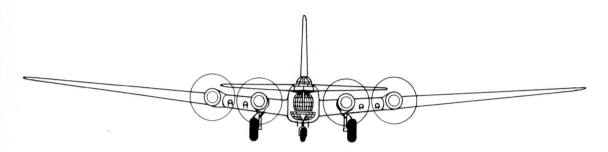

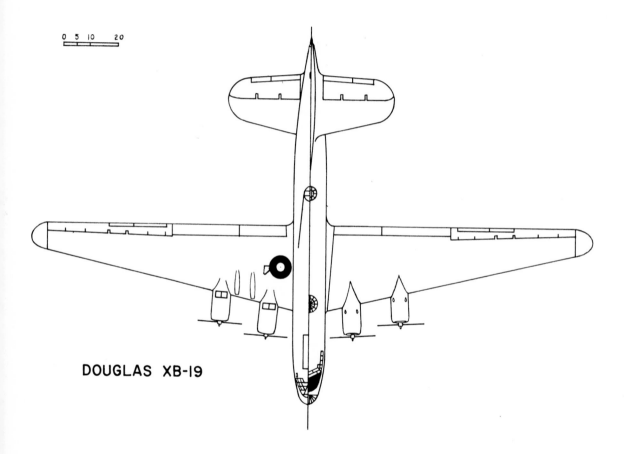

0 5 10   20

DOUGLAS XB-19

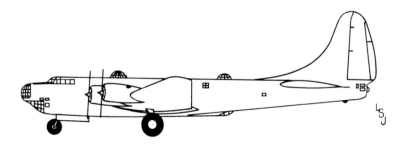

Fig. 58. Douglas XB-19.

Fig. 59. The great "Hemisphere Defender" XB-19A, at Davis-Monthan before it's destruction.

2,600 hp Allison V-3420-11 liquid cooled engines, advanced versions of the type originally intended for the plane, were installed. As the XB-19A, the top speed was increased to 265 mph and the service ceiling to 39,000 feet.

The XB-19's 212 foot wing had an area 4,285 square feet, the fuselage was 132 feet 4 inches long, and the rudder towered 42 feet. Fuel carried was 10,400 gallons. Cruising speed was 135 mph (185 mph with Allisons); landing speed was 70 mph. It could carry 16,000 pounds of bombs internally, and exterior racks could hold 20,000 pounds more. Range with 2,500 pounds of bombs was 7,710 miles.

Following an extensive testing program, the XB-19A was eventually used for cargo transport and in June of 1949, died on the scrap heap at Davis-Monthan Air Force Base.

Fig. 60. Note the double ailerons in this view. The XB-19 was the first bomber to use power boosted controls.

Fig. 61. Four Allison V-3420 engines were installed to increase performance. The plane was then redesignated XB-19A.

Fig. 62. Douglas' gigantic XB-19, shown here during an engine test, was so heavy the wheels cracked the pavement.

SIKORSKY
XBLR-3

Fig. 63. Wind tunnel model of the Sikorsky XBLR-3 at Langley Research Center of NACA, 1936.

In competition with the Douglas XBLR-2 (XB-19) was another four engine design, this one from the Sikorsky Aircraft Co. Although the XBLR-3 was never given a "B" designation, it is included here as it was the final proposal of the Long Range Bomber category.

The design was submitted to the Air Corps on February 29, 1936 and became known as restricted Project No. M5-35 or XBLR-3. Construction was begun on a wooden mockup, and in March of 1936 this was shown to the Air Corps. Following examination of the design, the XBLR-3 was rejected in favor of the Douglas plane and the Sikorsky project was cancelled.

The XBLR-3 wing span measured 205 feet with an aspect ratio of 9.11 and wing area of 4,614 square feet. Power source was to be four Allison XV-3420-1's of 1,600 horsepower driving three-bladed, 15 foot diameter constant speed props. Overall length was approximately 120 feet, height about 35 feet. The estimated gross weight was 119,977 pounds with a fuel load of 7,900 gallons.

Performance specifications of the Sikorsky bomber show a planned top speed of 220.5 mph and a normal cruising speed of 198 mph with a full load at sea level. A maximum range of 7,650 miles was to be reached at a cruise of 130 mph. Service ceiling is listed at 18,200 feet. The XBLR-3 was to have the capability of staying aloft for 62 hours.

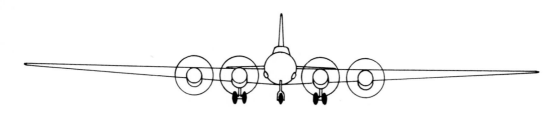

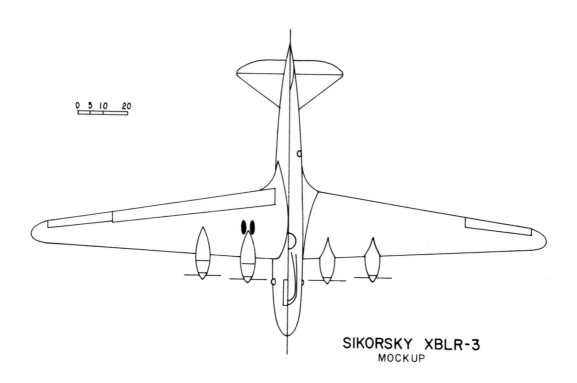

SIKORSKY XBLR-3
MOCKUP

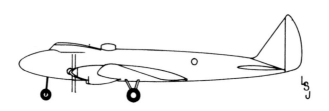

Fig. 64. Sikorsky XBLR-3.

Fig. 65. Checking the XBLR-3 model. This replica was 1/25th actual size of the proposed bomber.

BOEING
Y1B-20

Fig. 66. Scale model of the Boeing Model 316 heavy bomber project.

By the mid thirties, American bombing needs pointed to a "super bomber" type capable of a range of 4,000 miles with a bomb load of approximately 4,000 pounds. This plane would have to be a heavy four engine craft, and Boeing engineers offered their Model 316 in this category. Presented in March of 1938, the Model 316 was the result of an extensive re-evaluation of the underpowered XB-15.

The Model 316 was offered to the U.S.A.A.F. in several variations, the design illustrated being typical of the concept. By June, 1938, the project was given the designation Y1B-20. The proposed bomber incorporated pressurized crew quarters and four Wright GR-2600-A73 fourteen cylinder Cyclones of 1,350 horsepower. (Other variations offered Pratt & Whitney R-2180-5's with 1,400 horsepower.) A tricycle landing gear was adopted for the high-winged ship. The wing spanned 157 feet and had an area of 2,920 square feet. A crew of nine was to be carried within the 109 foot 2 inch fuselage. Height was 23 feet 4 inches. In this configuration the Y1B-20, or XB-20, weighed in at 50,680 pounds empty and 87,600 pounds gross. With a capacity for 4,450 gallons of fuel, the B-20 was to have a range of 4,000 miles. Service ceiling was 31,200 feet. The Wright powered Model 316 was given an estimated top speed of 258 mph and cruising speed of 242 mph. Proposed armament included four .50 cal. and three .30 cal. machine guns located singly in teardrop turrets. Bomb load ranged from sixteen 1,100 pounds bombs to forty-two 100 pound bombs.

Although a reversal of the "super bomber" concept by the Army led to the cancellation of the Y1B-20 program, the Boeing Company continued to develop and refine the original design which finally culminated in the famous B-29 Superfortress.

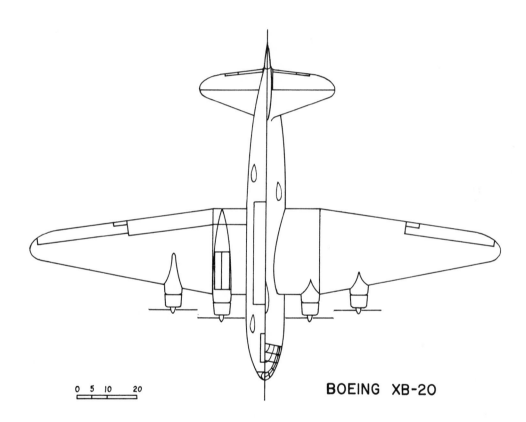

0 5 10   20

BOEING XB-20

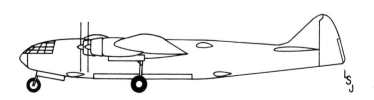

Fig. 67. Boeing XB-20.

Fig. 68. The XB-20 design was directly descended from the earlier XB-15 by Boeing.

NORTH AMERICAN
XB-21 DRAGON

Fig. 69. The North American Dragon showed a similarity to the B-18. Note supercharger on nacelle side, above landing gear.

For the design competition of March, 1937, North American offered their Model 21, a two engine midwing craft. A ball-type turret was located in the extreme nose, armed with one .30 cal. Browning gun. This arrangement placed the bombardier's compartment directly beneath that of the pilots'. Further single .30's were located in waist and ventral positions. A plexiglas turret topped the aft part of the fuselage, this also containing one gun. Eight crew members could be carried.

The Pratt & Whitney R-2180-1 Hornets were fitted with F-10 turbo superchargers and rated at 1,200 hp. The superchargers were tried at various locations on the nacelles during testing. Top speed was 220 mph with a cruising speed of 190 mph. A normal bomb load of 2,200 pounds could be flown 1,960 miles. The service ceiling was 25,000 feet and a rate of climb of 1,000 feet per minute was achieved. Integral fuel tanks held up to 2,400 gallons.

While undergoing evaluation trials, the upper turret was removed and a new all metal cap replaced the nose gun position. However, due to the higher cost of this plane over those already in production, the Air Corps purchased only the single prototype. Given the designation XB-21, it was assigned the serial number 38-485. Though a proposal was made to supply five planes for service trails, the project was dropped.

The XB-21 had a span of 95 feet. Length with the nose turret was 61 feet, and height was 17 feet. Empty and gross weights were 19,082 pounds and 27,253 pounds respectively. Overload weight was 40,000 pounds.

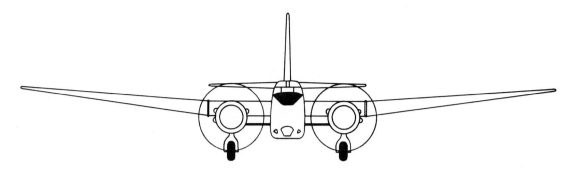

NO. AMERICAN XB-21

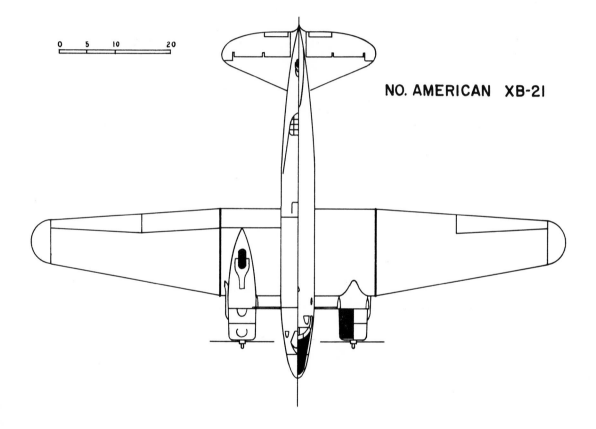

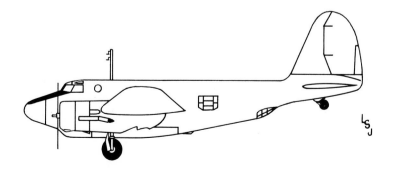

Fig. 70. North American XB-21 Dragon.

Fig. 71. North American's XB-21 Dragon at Wright Field after turrets had been removed.

Fig. 72. High production costs doomed the XB-21, North American's first bomber project.

DOUGLAS
B-23 DRAGON

Fig. 73. The Douglas B-23 Dragon was a continued development of the DC-3 transport design.

Appearing in place of the cancelled XB-22 was a much cleaner design from the Douglas drafting boards. Another development of the DC-3 transport, the B-23 showed a family likeness to the earlier B-18. Gone, however, was the shark nose and deep paunch. The landing gear was completely hidden behind large doors when retracted, and the first tail turret to be used on an American Army bomber sat beneath the high rudder. The nose turret was removed leaving a spacious bombardier's compartment. (It was not felt necessary to defend the nose of the faster aircraft.)

The 38 B-23's built were financed by funds transferred from the B-18A contract and all were production aircraft. There was no prototype. The first B-23 (serial number 39-27) flew on July 27, 1939, nine months after it was proposed. In spite of the obvious improvements shown by the aircraft, they did not keep pace with aerodynamic advances now apparent in the art. By the time the last B-23 was delivered in September, 1940, the Dragon was obsolete. Twelve were converted to UC-67 transports, while the remainder saw limited service as patrol planes. Eventually, they became trainers or glider tugs.

Two Wright R-2600-3 Cyclones, giving a total of 3,200 hp, were used to give a top speed of 282 mph. A range of 1,445 miles was achieved with 4,000 pounds of bombs. Cruising speed was 210 mph, and the B-23 landed at 80 mph. Service ceiling was 31,600 feet. Empty weight was 19,059 pounds; gross weight was 26,500 pounds.

Dimensions were: span, 92 feet; length, 58 feet 4 inches; height, 18 feet 6 inches. Wing area was 993 square feet.

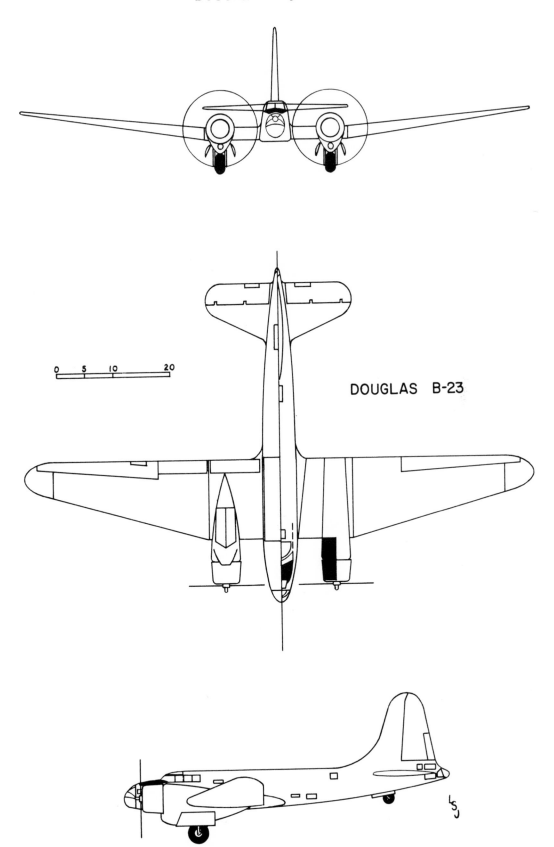

Fig. 74. Douglas B-23 Dragon.

Fig. 75. In spite of many advanced features in the B-23, it was obsolete before reaching service status. Note tail turret.

Fig. 76. The B-23 was considered fast enough that no forward armament was necessary. The tail turret was a new innovation on American aircraft.

CONVAIR
YB-24 LIBERATOR

Fig. 77. The XB-24 made its initial flight on December 29, 1939.

At the request of the U.S.A.A.F., in September, 1938, the Consolidated Aircraft Co. (later Convair) began design studies for a heavy bomber with a performance exceeding the Boeing B-17. The result of the project, known as Consolidated Model 32, was a squat, four engine design with a shoulder mounted wing for greater payload capacity and two large vertical stabilizers. A smooth, unbroken nose line, of the type later to become familiar on the Boeing B-29, was rejected before the prototype was completed. The location of the high lift Davis wing permitted easy access to the bomb compartment, which was covered by two pairs of hinged panels that slid upward along the fuselage to allow the release of 8,800 pounds of bombs.

So promising was the design, that before the new XB-24 was completed, seven YB-24's were ordered, and before the prototype had flown, thirty-eight B-24's were authorized. On December 29, 1939, the four Pratt & Whitney R-1830 -33 1,200 hp Twin Wasps carried the XB-24 (serial number 39-680) into the air for its maiden flight. However, flight tests showed a top speed of only 273 mph instead of the 311 mph estimated, so four supercharged R-1830-41's were installed, fixed slots in the wing removed, and the more acceptable top speed of 310 mph was attained. The plane became the XB-24B after these changes.

The seven YB-24's had a top speed of 275 mph, and aside from the addition of de-icer boots and camouflage paint, were otherwise identical to the XB-24. They had a wing area of 1,048 square feet, a span of 110 feet, length of 63 feet 9 inches, and stood 18 feet 8 inches on tricycle gear --- the B-24 being the first production bomber with this wheel arrangement. Empty weight was 27,500 pounds, gross weight was 38,360 pounds, and maximum weight, with 3,000 gallons of fuel, came to 46,400 pounds. Cruising speed was 186 mph, landing at 90 mph. Service ceiling was 31,500 feet, and

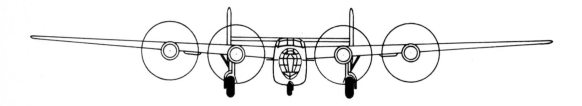

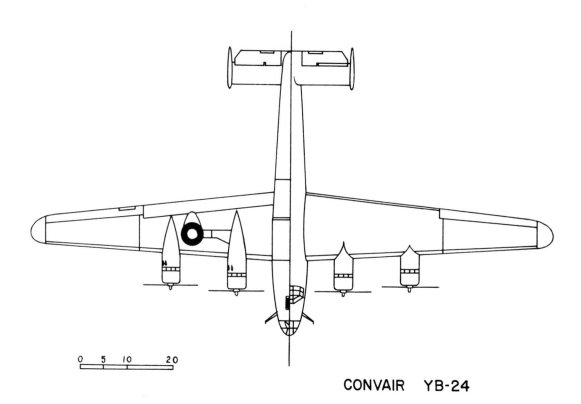

0   5   10   20

CONVAIR   YB-24

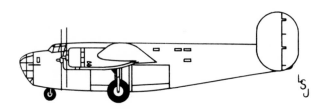

Fig. 78. Convair YB-24 Liberator.

Fig. 79. Convair XB-24. Note prop spinners and absence of gun turrets.

maximum range was 4,700 miles. Armament consisted of one .30 cal. Browning machine gun located in the nose, a single gun on each side of the fuselage, two more above and below, and a sixth one could be fired through a hatch in the tail.

By June, 1941, nine of the B-24A's were in the hands of the Army -- the remainder of the original 38 ordered being converted to later models during construction. The "A"'s were armed with six .50's and a turret in the tail carried dual .30's.

Nine B-24C's followed, adding a Martin upper turret with twin .50 cal. guns and a Consolidated turret in the tail with the same protection. Length was increased to 66 feet 4 inches and top speed to 313 mph.

Production of the B-24D was relegated to Convair and Douglas, and Ford joined them in the assembly of the E model.

One B-24D became the XB-24F to test thermal de-icing. Four hundred thirty B-24G's were produced by North American.

All of the latter models were basically the same with only minor variations in power or armament. B-24G's empty weight was 36,500 pounds with a gross of 41,000 pounds. Armament included ten .50 cal. guns with 4,700 rounds of ammunition, and a bomb load of 12,800 pounds could be carried. Length was 67 feet 2 inches. Crews varied from eight to ten men. Top speed was 290 mph, landing at 95 mph. Engines were R-1830-65's of 1,200 hp with supercharging.

The different types were produced in the following quantities: B-24D - 2,738; B-24E - 791; B-24F - 1 converted; B-24G - 430.

Several hundred B-24's of various types were sold to the British, from whom the popular name Liberator was derived.

Fig. 80. Consolidated (later Convair) YB-24.

Fig. 81. A Convair B-24D-30, one of a block of eighty.

CONVAIR
B-24J LIBERATOR

Fig. 82. One of 100 B-24J-145's built by Convair, San Diego.

The first major external change of the B-24 lines appeared on the twenty-sixth B-24G, when a new nose was designed to include a power turret containing two .50 cal. guns for frontal protection. This more effective forward arrangement increased the length to 67 feet 2 inches. The Sperry ball turret became standard equipment on this and following models.

The B-24J Liberator was the variation produced in the largest quantity; a total of 6,678 being constructed. It was so similar to the G and H models that the latter were modified to become B-24J's by changing the autopilot and bombsight. Armed with twin .50 cal. Brownings in the nose, upper, lower ball, waist, and tail turrets, a total of 5,200 rounds of ammunition were carried. The top speed

of 290 mph was provided by four Pratt & Whitney supercharged R-1830-65's with 1,200 hp each. Cruise was 215 mph and landing speed was 95 mph with its Fowler flaps. Rate of climb was 1,025 feet per minute, and service ceiling was 28,000 feet. Empty, the B-24J weighed 36,500 pounds and grossed out at 56,000 pounds. Maximum range extended 3,700 miles. Span was 110 feet; wing area, 1,048 square feet; length, 67 feet 2 inches; height, 18 feet. Fuel capacity was 3,614 gallons.

The 1,667 B-24L's and 2,593 B-24M models varied only slightly in armament fixtures from their predecessors. Several B-24's were used as transports under the Air Force designation of C-87 Liberator Express and a few became C-109 fuel tankers.

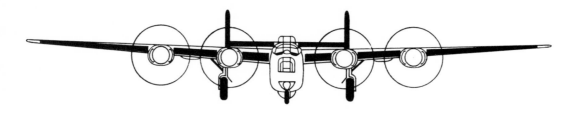

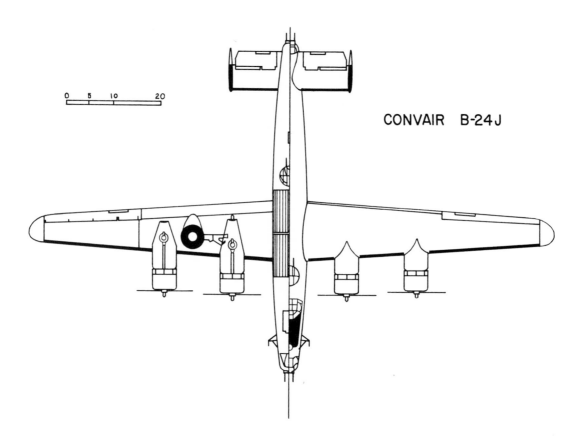

CONVAIR   B-24J

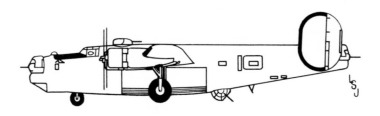

Fig. 83. Convair B-24J Liberator.

Fig. 84. The 42nd B-24M-45 from San Diego.

Fig. 85. A biplane B-24! This B-24M 30 CO (44-42417) of the 459th Bombardment group mounted a stubby wing shaped radome beneath the fuselage. This structure actually contributed to the lift of the aircraft, but caused adverse flying characteristics.

CONVAIR - FORD
XB-24N LIBERATOR

Fig. 86. The single tail configuration of the XB-24N improved performance.

The most radical departure from the original B-24 design was the single tail XB-24N built by Ford. Shortly after the B-24 became operational, it was theorized that a more conventional tail assembly would give the plane better performance. To test this idea, a B-24D was modified to this configuration. In addition, four 1,350 hp R-1830-75 engines by Pratt & Whitney were installed. With the plane designated XB-24K, the new tail proved the theories to be correct, as stability, speed, and rate of climb increased greatly. As a result of the tests, it was determined that all subsequent B-24's would be of the single fin and rudder variety. In April, 1944, Ford began building an improved single tail version -- the XB-24N. Completely dispensing with the existing B-24 nose and empennage, the new ship was by far the cleanest of the type. A ball turret, surrounded by plexiglas windows, was mounted on the front of the tapered nose. The single tail, slimmer than that on the B-24K, reached a height of 26 feet 9 inches. A new turret was located beneath the rudder. In May, 1945, the XB-24N (serial number 44-48753) was accepted by the Air Force, but by the time Liberator production ceased, only seven YB-24N aircraft had been completed. They were powered by the same R-1830-75's as used on the XB-24K, and had a top speed of 294 mph, cruising at 213 mph. They could climb to 20,000 feet in 29 minutes and carry 5,000 pounds of bombs for 2,000 miles. Maximum range was 3,500 miles. As in the others of the Liberator series, they carried a ten man crew.

The following specifications pertain to the XB-24N: span, 110 feet; length, 67 feet 2 inches; height, 26 feet 9 inches; wing area, 1,048 square feet; empty weight, 38,300 pounds; gross weight, 56,000 pounds; maximum weight, 65,000 pounds; maximum fuel capacity, 3,614 gallons.

Let us point out that the XB-24N was not related to the single tail PB4Y-2 Privateer used by the Navy. The latter was a completely different development of the basic B-24 design.

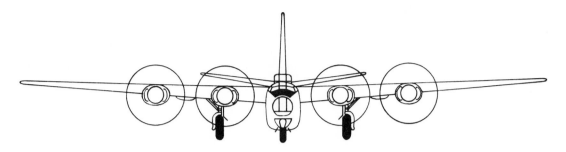

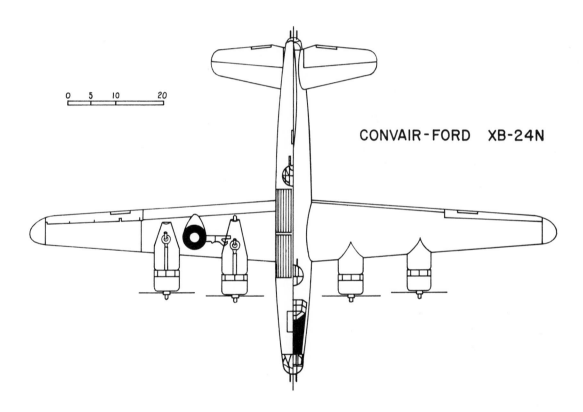

CONVAIR-FORD XB-24N

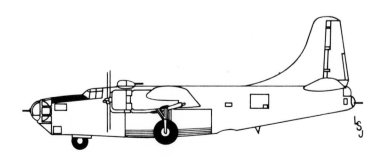

Fig. 87. Conviar-Ford XB-24N Liberator.

Fig. 88. Note the new type power tail turret adopted for the XB-24N.

*Fig. 89. A Convair PB4Y-2 Privateer. This plane was a single tail version of the B-24 built
for the Navy.*

NORTH AMERICAN
NA-40-2

Fig. 90. North American NA-40 with two P & W Twin Wasps.

Although no "B" designation was assigned to the NA-40, it is included in this history because of its direct relationship to the North American B-25. The NA-40 was North American's offering to a 1938 Air Corps request for a twin engine attack bomber. The all metal plane had the relatively new tricycle landing gear and a narrow fuselage, seating the pilot and co-pilot in tandem. Provisions were made for a crew of five and 1,200 pounds of bombs. A fuel capacity of 476 gallons fed the two 1,100 horsepower Pratt & Whitney R-1830-S6C3-G Twin Wasp engines. Gross weight was 19,500 pounds.

In January, 1939, the NA-40 was first flown, but the top speed of 265 mph was considered insufficient. A month later, as the NA-40-2, it again took to the air, but power was increased to 1,300 hp per engine with a pair of Wright R-2600-A71 Cyclones. The new engines boosted the top speed to 285 mph, and the gross weight to 21,000 pounds.

In March, the NA-40-2 was delivered to Wright Field for Air Corps testing. During this program, the plane showed outstanding performance characteristics, and up to seven further versions of the design were proposed. Unfortunately, the development of the NA-40 was halted when one of the test pilots lost control of the aircraft during a landing approach and, although the crew escaped, the single NA-40 prototype was destroyed by fire following the crash.

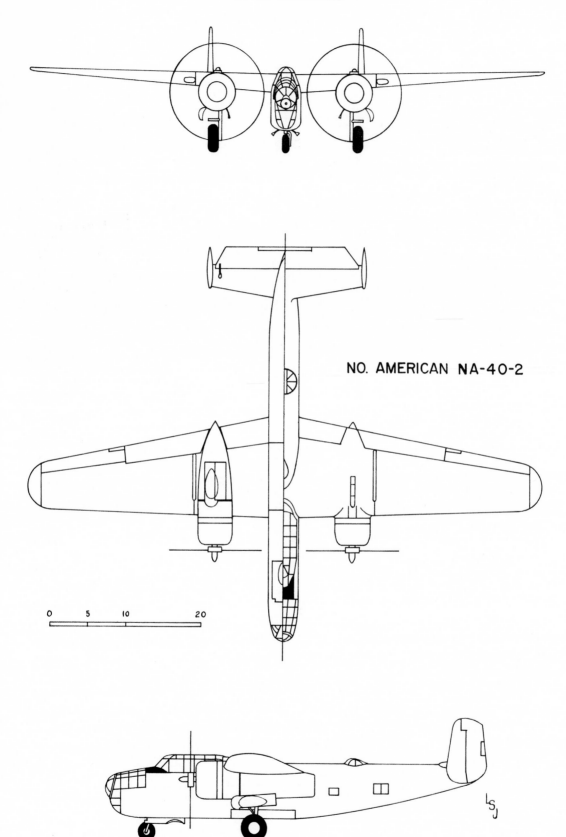

NO. AMERICAN NA-40-2

0   5   10   20

Fig. 91. North American NA-40-2.

Fig. 92. The NA-40-2 with the more powerful Wright Cyclones.

As an attack bomber, the NA-40 was to carry one .30 cal. M-2 machine gun in a rotating nose blister, one in the dorsal turret, and another firing through the rear floor. Two fixed .30's were planned for installation in each wing.

As the NA-40-2 (or NA-40-B), the plane weighed empty 13,961 pounds and had a gross weight of 21,000 pounds. Service ceiling was 25,000 feet and range was 1,200 miles. The wing had a span of 66 feet, fuselage length was 48 feet 3 inches, and height was 15 feet 2 inches. Wing area was 598½ square feet.

The NA-40 did not receive a military designation or serial number.

NORTH AMERICAN
B-25H MITCHELL

Fig. 93. One of the first nine B-25's with the unbroken dihedral.

The B-25 Mitchell, named after the General who so staunchly advocated greater airpower, was actually a greatly improved development of the NA-40. North American Model NA-62 was the result of increasing the payload and performance of the earlier design. To accomodate 2,400 pounds of bombs, the fuselage was widened. The co-pilot was then placed beside the pilot.

The first plane of this type to fly was a production B-25, as the design was ordered from the drawing board due to the success of the NA-40. First flight date was August 19, 1940. This ship was powered by two Wright R-2600-9 Cyclone engines delivering a total of 3,400 horsepower. Top speed was 322 mph. Following difficulties with directional stability during the bombing run, the dihedral in the outer wing panels was eliminated on the tenth and all following B-25's.

The first twenty-five B-25's were armed with a .30 cal. Browning in the nose and one each in waist positions. The tail was protected by a single .50. As the B-25 saw operational service, many modifications were undertaken to increase its firepower. Most notable among these was the adoption of the 75 mm M-4 cannon. The 900 pound, 9 foot 6 inch gun was introduced on the B-25G and was the largest weapon ever installed in an American bomber. The plexiglas nose of the plane was replaced by a shorter "solid" type with two .50 cal. Brownings fixed to fire coincidentally with the cannon. The "G" had a dorsal turret located above a retractable belly turret amidship.

The succeeding B-25H had the lower turret removed and the top gun position moved forward. Firepower in the nose was increased by the addition of two more .50 cal. machine guns above a lighter 75 mm cannon, and four "package" guns were mounted to the side of the fuselage below the cockpit. A new turret in the tail held twin .50's. To compensate for the removal of the ventral turret, two plexiglas blisters were located on the fuselage sides aft of the wing. These each had one .50 cal. gun.

The B-25H Mitchell was powered by two Wright R-2600-13 or -29 Cyclones with mechanical superchargers. Each

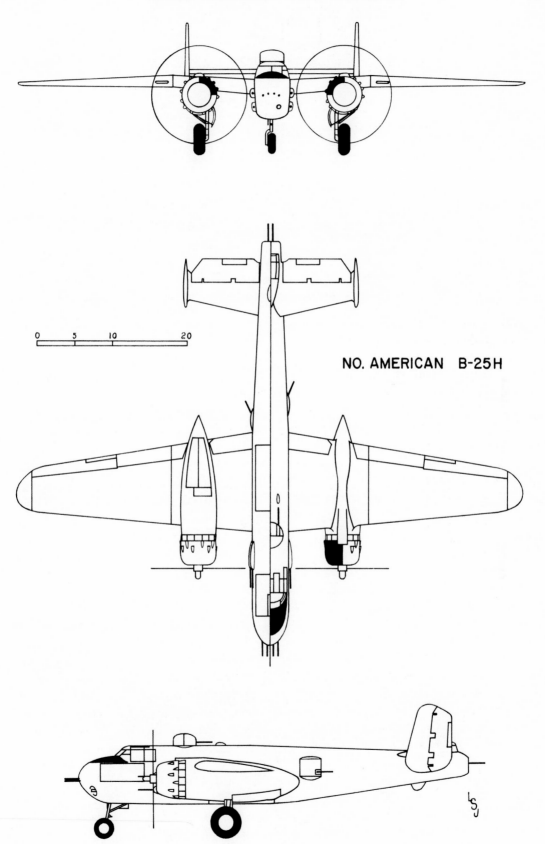

0 5 10 20

NO. AMERICAN B-25H

Fig. 94. North American B-25H Mitchell.

Fig. 95. A reconstruction of the B-25C used by General Doolittle on his historic raid. The The original aircraft was modified in secret and no photographs were made.

engine gave 1,700 horsepower normal which could be boosted to 1,850 hp for war emergency. Top speed was 275 mph at a gross weight of 33,500 pounds, with a cruising speed of 230 mph. Landing speed was 105 mph. Empty weight was 19,975 pounds. Three thousand pounds. of bombs could be carried and underwing mountings held eight 5 inch high velocity air rockets. Range was 1,350 miles with a maximum of 974 gallons of fuel. Span was 67 feet 7 inches, length was 51 feet (models with the plexiglas nose were 52 feet 11 inches long), height 15 feet 9 inches, wing area 610 square feet. Service ceiling was 23,800 feet with a climb to 15,000 feet in 19 minutes. The B-25J, final model of the series, reverted back to the plexiglas nose.

Unquestionably, the most famous exploit of this bomber was the successful carrier-based attack on Japan. Though

Fig. 96. A B-25H-10, the last of 1,000 of the "H" series. By order of the Air Force, the names painted on the aircraft by the workers remained throughout the life of the plane. This plane was nicknamed "Bones".

Fig. 97. A B-25H-5 Mitchell.

all 16 planes were lost, it did prove the strength and adaptability of American bombers.

Of a total of 9,815 Mitchells procurred by the Air Corps, 24 were delivered as B-25's, 40 were B-25A's, 119 were B-25B, 1,619 were B-25C, 2,290 were B-25D, 405 were B-25G, 1,000 were B-25H, and 4,318 were B-25J. The XB-25E and F were "C"'s modified with thermal deicers.

Fig. 98. North American B-25C with retractable lower turret.

MARTIN
B-26B MARAUDER

Fig. 99. One of eight Martin Marauder B-26C-5-MO's built at the Martin plant in Omaha, Nebr.

One of the most controversial airplanes of its time, the Martin Model 179, or B-26 Marauder, none the less proved to be an exceptional performer. As Martin's answer to an Air Corps performance specification in January, 1939, the design was immediately ordered into full production. The first unit (A. F. serial number 40-1361) was flown on November 25, 1940, and very little modification was ·found necessary, although the plane demanded a great deal of respect from its pilot.

The two Pratt & Whitney R-2800-5 Double Wasp engines mounted in front of needle pointed nacelles, gave the B-26 a 3,700 hp pull to a speed of 315 mph. The thirteen and one-half foot, four bladed propellers were the first used on this type of American aircraft. Bomb load came to 3,000 pounds, and service ceiling was 25,000 feet. Fuel capacity was 962 gallons which gave a range of 1,000 miles. But the small wing, with a span of 65 feet and an area of 602 square feet to carry a gross weight of 27,200 pounds, was a source of trouble. The B-26 had an unusually high wing loading of 50 pounds per square foot. This fact led to much apprehension following its introduction to the service, due to the high loss of aircraft during training. The wing span was increased to 71 feet and the area to 659 square feet on the six hundred forty-second B-26B.

The "B" was powered by two Pratt & Whitney R-2800-42 or -43 engines with a rating of 2,000 hp. Increased weight to 24,000 pounds empty and 31,000 pounds gross slowed the top speed to 282 mph and raised the landing speed to 135 mph. Rate of climb was 1,500 feet per minute. A total of twelve .50 cal. machine guns armed the B-26B following the addition of four "package" guns on the fuselage.

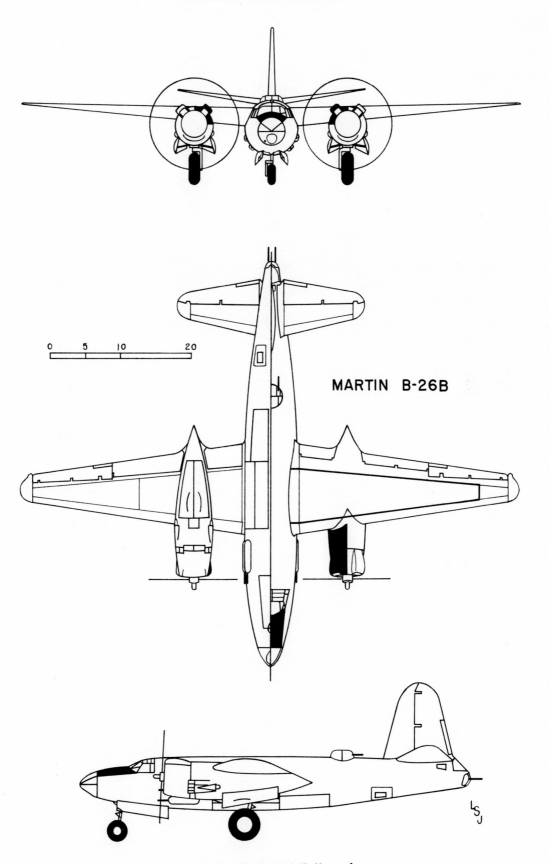

MARTIN B-26B

Fig. 100. Martin B-26B Marauder.

Fig. 101. A B-26G-5-MA showing increased wing incidence and package guns.

Three thousand pounds of bombs were carried 1,150 miles. Maximum range was 2,800 miles. Service ceiling was 23,500 feet.

The Marauder had an unusual bomb bay arrangement consisting of folding doors in the front and conventional hinged type in the rear. On later models, shackles were fitted to the keel between the bomb doors for holding a 2,000 pound aerial torpedo.

In a final attempt to reduce take-off and landing speeds, the B-26F and G wing incidence angle was increased three and a half degrees, but the most noticeable result was a more level flight attitude.

The final tally of B-26's produced amounted to 5,157 -- B-26B's accounting for 1,883 of these. The basic B-26 dimensions were span, 71 feet (65 feet on short wing models); length, 56 feet, extending to 58 feet 3 inches with modified tail turret; height, 21 feet 6 inches. The accompanying three-view drawing depicts a B-26B-55 with the 58 foot length.

MARTIN
XB-27

Fig. 102. Model of Martin XB-27 depicted in flight.

In August, 1939, the Air Corps released specification XC-214 for a high altitude medium bomber. The Martin 182 was projected to fill this position, and the design was given the Air Corps identification XB-27.

Although intended to be a pressurized adaptation of the Martin B-26, the resemblance was confined mainly to the tail structure. The location of the cockpit just forward of the wing gave the XB-27 an appearance more like a fighter than a bomber. Main units of the tricycle landing gear retracted outward into the wing, which, for high altitude operation, had a span of 84 feet and an area of 750 square feet. Overall length was to be 60 feet 9 inches, with a height of 20 feet.

It was planned to power the XB-27

with two Pratt & Whitney R-2800-9 Double Wasp engines whose combined rating of 4,200 hp were to result in a top speed of 376 mph. Service ceiling was estimated at 33,500 feet, and range at 2,900 miles with 4,000 pounds of bombs. Proposed armament located one .30 cal. gun in the nose, the rear of the cockpit fairing, and a moveable fixture amidships which could be fired downward or through ports in the fuselage side. One .50 cal. gun was to be placed in the tail position. Weights of 23,125 pounds empty and 32,970 pounds gross were calculated. Maximum crew would be seven, and fuel capacity was 1,306 gallons.

The XB-27 did not progress beyond the blueprint stage and the designation was bypassed.

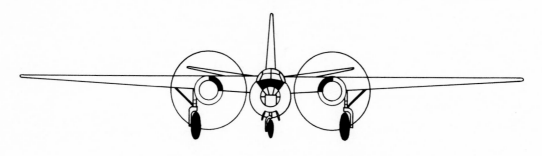

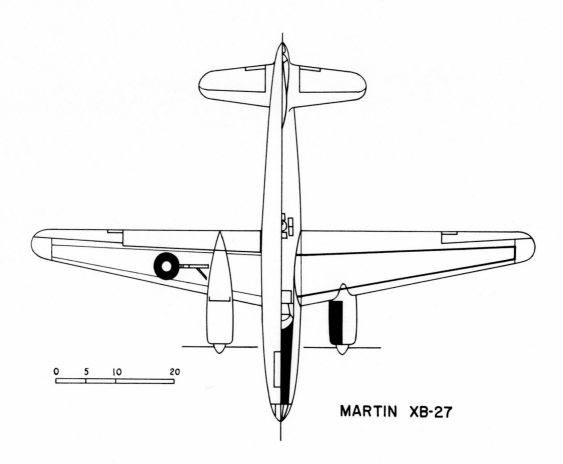

MARTIN XB-27

0   5   10   20

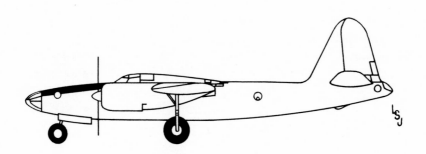

Fig. 103. Martin XB-27.

Fig. 104. A model of the unbuilt XB-27 high altitude bomber.

NORTH AMERICAN
XB-28

Fig. 105. The second plane was designated XB-28A and was modified for photo reconnaissance work.

In response to the Air Corps need for a high altitude supplement to the North American B-25, this company produced their model NA-63, or XB-28. The first of the two test aircraft (serial number 40-3056) flew in April, 1942 -- twenty-six months after the order was placed. The XB-28 bore no similarity at all to the earlier B-25, having a circular fuselage with a large bulbous empennage topped with a single vertical stabilizer. The plane was powered by two Pratt & Whitney R-2800-27 2,000 hp Wasps with C-2 superchargers driving four-bladed propellers in opposite directions to reduce torque. Remote control ventral and dorsal turrets held pairs of .50 cal. guns, as did the remotely operated tail stinger. The crew of five was seated in the cabin which was pressurized by a pair of exhaust driven "Roots" blowers on the engines. The gunners sat just behind the cockpit aiming and firing the remote control guns by use of periscopic sights protruding above and below the fuselage. Four thousand pounds of bombs could be dropped from a service ceiling of 34,600 feet. Top speed was 372 mph with a cruising speed of 255 mph -- far above contemporary production aircraft.

Lower altitude bombing techniques had developed to such an extent that it was not considered necessary to reduce production on the operational types in favor of the XB-28. However, recognition of the high altitude reconnaissance potential of the aircraft led to the construction of the second airframe (40-3058) as the XB-28A for photo work.

The XB-28 had a wing spanning 72 feet 7 inches, with an area of 676 square feet. The tubular fuselage was 56 feet 5 inches long and the rudder was 14 feet high. Empty and loaded weights were 25,575 pounds and 35,740 pounds each. Maximum gallons of gas carried was 1,508. Range was 2,040 miles cruising at 255 mph.

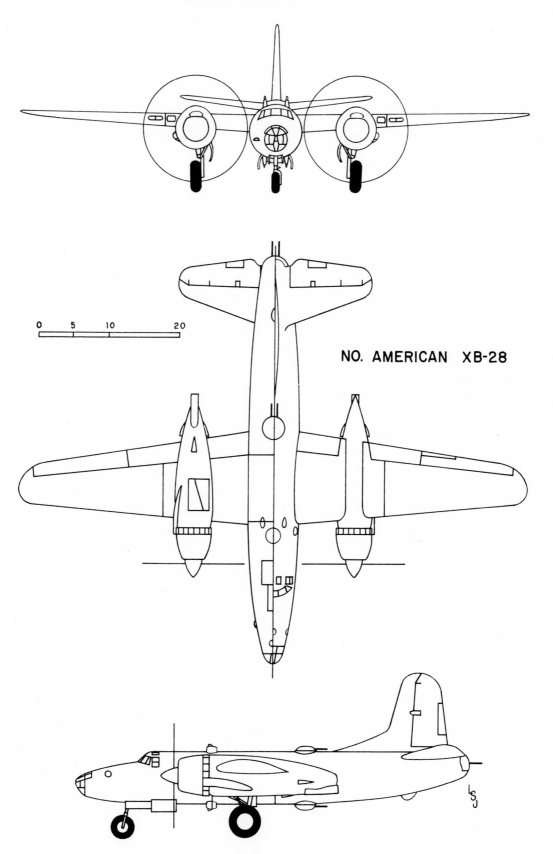

NO. AMERICAN XB-28

0   5   10   20

Fig. 106. North American XB-28.

Fig. 107. North American's pressurized XB-28 high altitude bomber (serial number 40-3056).

BOEING
B-29 SUPERFORTRESS

Fig. 108. A Bell built B-29-30-BA from their plant in Atlanta, Georgia.

"B-29'S RAID TOKYO"! To many people, these headlines were the first announcement that America actually possessed the long dreamed of "super bomber". And super it was, by all comparative standards. Its four Wright R-3350-23 eighteen cylinder Cyclone engines each gave 2,430 horsepower for war emergency and 8,198 gallons of fuel enabled it to carry up to 20,000 pounds of bombs 3,250 miles and return. The B-29 had a range greater than any other bomber of its day. With a pressurized fuselage and two superchargers on each engine, the new ship had a service ceiling of 31,850 feet. The Superfortress, whose name was adapted from it's smaller brother, the B-17, was also the heaviest bomber in the skies, having an empty weight of 70,140 pounds and a gross of 110,000

pounds; and a top speed of 358 mph made it one of the fastest.

The B-29, or Boeing Model 345, was first ordered in August, 1940, and the XB-29 (41-002) was first airborne on September 21, 1942. The prototype aircraft was devoid of its protective armament in an attempt to speed flight testing. The second XB-29 (41-003) flew on December 28, 1942, but was destroyed in a fiery crash along with its crew the following February. However, the potential of the aircraft was a proven fact and production was ordered in spite of this, and other temporary setbacks.

The fire control system of the B-29 was the most advanced yet. Four gun turrets with twin .50 cal. machine guns were remotely controlled from within the fuselage. Forward protection was afforded

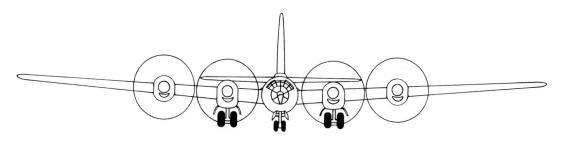

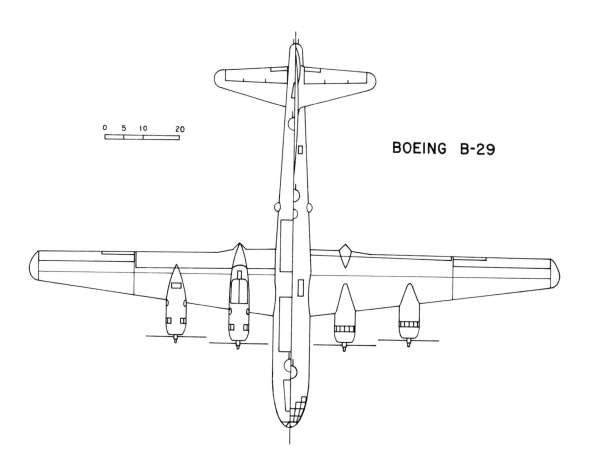

0   5   10   20

BOEING B-29

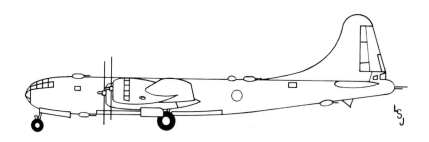

Fig. 109. Boeing B-29 Superfortress.

Fig. 110. A B-29A-1-BO (42-93837) banks gracefully around Boeing's "trademark", Mt. Rainer, Washington.

by the upper and lower positions just behind the cockpit. A manned tail position offered the bite of a 20 mm M-2 cannon in addition to the twin .50's to anyone venturing too close.

The B-29A had the 141 foot 3 inch wing span increased to 142 feet 3 inches by a change in the wing center structure; and on later "A"'s, the 20 mm cannon was either omitted or replaced by a third .50 cal machine gun. Wing area on the B-29 was 1,736 square feet. The length of 99 feet and height of 29 feet 7 inches remained the same throughout the series. One thousand, one hundred sixteen B-29 A's were built by Boeing.

Bell Aircraft constructed three hundred eleven B-29's with R-3350-51's of 2,200 hp. This version was the fastest of the Superfortress types, having a top speed of 367 mph. The entire quantity of B-29's built by Boeing, Bell, and Martin was 3,970 at the conclusion of production in 1945.

In spite of its excellence as a bomber, the B-29's performance will always be overshadowed by the fact that it was the aircraft which ushered in the Atomic Age on August 6, 1945, with the destruction of Hiroshima, Japan. However, it was in fact, just another routine mission for a plane of tremendous capabilities.

LOCKHEED
XB-30

Fig. 111. Photo of model XB-30, planned bomber version of Constellation transport.

Lockheed Aircraft Company entered the 1940 heavy bombardment contest with a design, which though not accepted as a bomber, was soon a familiar sight as the famous Constellation transport. Identified by the Air Corps as the XB-30, it was a proposed adaptation of the new Model 49 airliner then under construction. A lengthened nose was to be covered with plexiglas panels for the bombardier with the rear of the fuselage extended for a turret holding a pair of .50 cal. machine guns and one 20mm cannon. Four remote turrets broke the clean profile, each armed with pairs of .50's and aimed through periscopes.

Four 2,200 hp R-3350-13 Wright Cyclones were expected to give a 450 mph top speed and a service ceiling of 40,000 feet. The range was to be 3,380 miles at a cruise speed of 240 mph. Fuel load was 18,085 gallons; bomb capacity was 16,000 pounds. Empty weight was given as 51,725 pounds and gross weight came to 86,000 pounds. Useful load was 28,909 pounds. Seven men were to make up the crew.

Dimensions of the XB-30 were the same as the Constellation with the exception of the lengthened fuselage. Span was 123 feet, length was 104 feet 3 inches, and the triple fins stood 23 feet 9.5 inches above the ground. Wing area was 1,650 square feet.

Although the design was later proven versatile as a transport, the XB-30 was rejected in favor of the B-29 for a long range bomber and no aircraft were built.

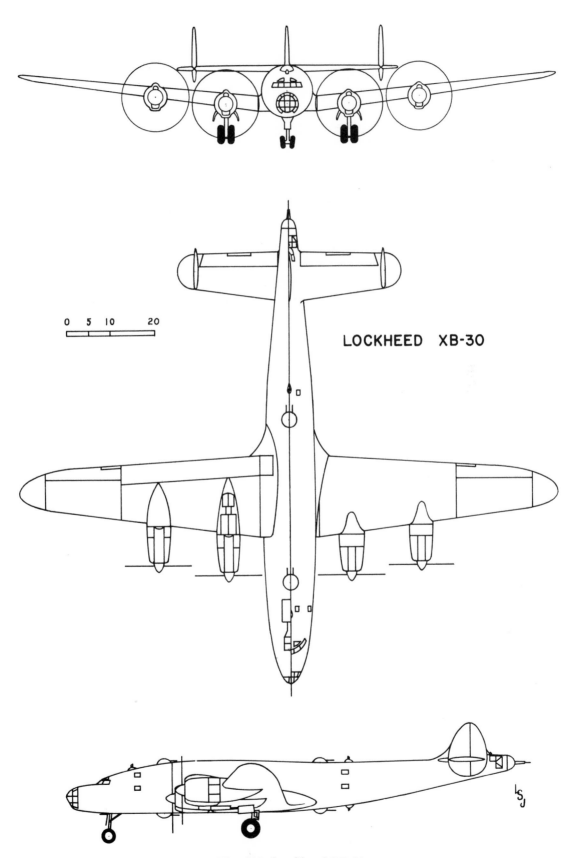

0 5 10   20

LOCKHEED XB-30

Fig. 112. Lockheed XB-30.

Fig. 113. The XB-30's extended tail was to hold two .50's and one 20mm cannon.

DOUGLAS
XB-31 (MODEL 423)

Fig. 114. The model 423 would have been only slightly smaller than the XB-19.

When aircraft engineers enter a design competition, many deviations in the original concept can produce a wide variety of shapes and dimensions before a final airframe is accepted or rejected. This is particularly true in the case of the Douglas XB-31 project.

In the same contest that spawned the B-29, Douglas was permitted to develop a design study under the Air Corps label of XB-31. There was in fact, no XB-31 design. This blanket title covered the various engineering studies. The Douglas Model 423 shown here is typical of the studies which originally began as a bomber development of the commercial DC-4.

The Douglas XB-31 Model 423 was offered during the latter part of 1941 as a long range bomber of very advanced concept. Its 207 foot wing span was exceeded only by the XB-19, and that by only five feet. The wing area was 3,300 square feet. The length of the fuselage was 117 feet 3 inches -- just 3 inches shorter than the DC-4 wing span. Height was 40 feet 5 inches. Four new 3,000 hp engines, known then as X-Wasps, but later as Pratt & Whitney R-4360 Wasp Majors, were specified to turn the 25 foot, three-bladed propellers. Fuel tanks held 13,000 gallons, and the 450 gallons of oil carried exceeded the total fuel capacity of some of the early bombers of the 1930's.

The crew of eight was to be housed in

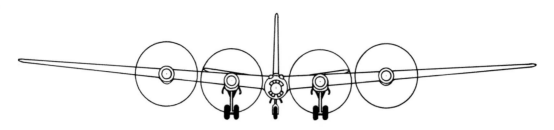

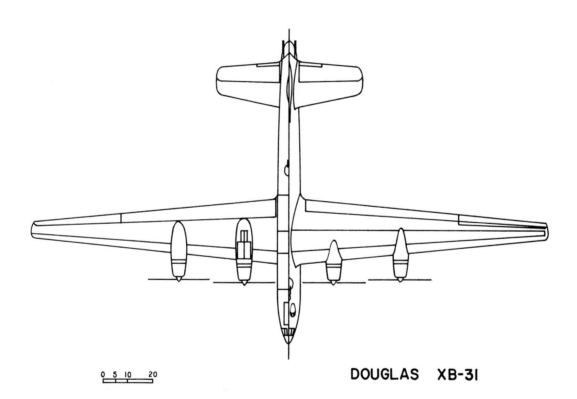

DOUGLAS XB-3I

0 5 10   20

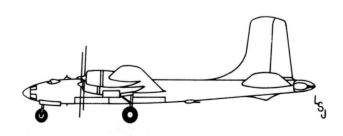

Fig. 115. Douglas XB-31.

Fig. 116. A model of the Douglas XB-31, design number 423.

a perfectly streamlined pressurized fuselage -- pilot and co-pilot stations topped by two small bubble canopies. Immediately behind the twin cockpits was the remote sighting station for two barbettes with dual .50 cal. machine guns. Tail protection was in the form of two 37 mm cannons, also remotely controlled. The double bomb bay had a capacity of 25,000 pounds. Empty weight of this XB-31 study was estimated as 109,200 pounds, gross at 176,000 pounds. Overload weight was to be 198,000 pounds. No further performance characteristics are specified on this proposal.

Even though the design did not proceed beyond the study category, it is apparent that some of the features influenced later Douglas aircraft. For example, the Douglas C-74 transport featured the double bubble canopies, and the Model 423 tail assembly appears in a smaller scale on the Invader attack bomber.

CONVAIR
XB-32

Fig. 117. Many features of the B-24 are apparent in this view of the XB-32.

A fourth contender for the "Super-bomber" title fared better than the XB-30 and XB-31 proposals. However, the development of the Convair XB-32 (Model 33) was pushed only as an insurance of a heavy bomber in the event of a failure of the B-29 program. A contract for development was awarded on September 6, 1940, and the first XB-32 (41-141) started flight tests on September 7, 1942. The shoulder wing and twin rudders of the prototype left no doubt as to its relationship with the smaller Convair B-24. A crash after some thirty flights halted testing until the second prototype (41-142) could be completed. The number two XB-32 first flew on July 2, 1943.

These planes were equipped with cockpit pressurization and retractable gun turrets in the fuselage, which were remotely operated. A manned position was also provided in the tail. A total armament of fourteen .50 cal. guns were fed 7,000 rounds while two 20 mm cannons were given 200 rounds. The tandem bomb bays were covered by the same type of sliding, interlocking panels as the B-24 and had a capacity of 20,000 pounds. The four powerplants used were Wright R-3350-13 Cyclones of 2,200 hp turning three-bladed props. A top speed of 376 mph was attributed to the XB-32 which landed at 96 mph. Service ceiling was 30,700 feet. Normal range was 4,450 miles at a cruising speed of 250 mph. A crew of from six to eleven was carried.

Wing span of the XB-32 was 135 feet; area was 1,422 square feet. Length was

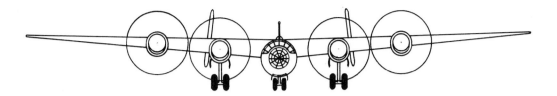

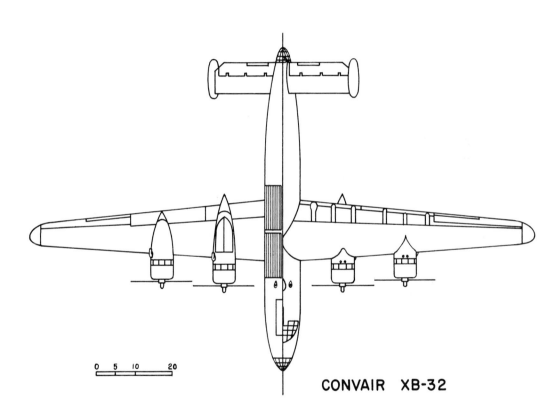

0 5 10 20

CONVAIR XB-32

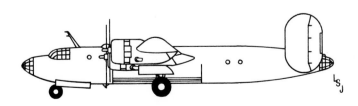

Fig. 118. Convair XB-32 Dominator.

Fig. 119. The YB-32 had the tall single rudder used by the production models.

83 feet, and height reached 20 feet 10 inches. Weight ranged from 64,960 pounds empty to a gross of 101,662 pounds. Maximum permissable weight was 113,500 pounds.

On November 9, 1943, the third B-32 took to the air. This one was refitted with a single fin that towered to 32 feet above the plane and redesignated YB-32 (41-18336). This plane, while retaining much of the appearance of the two XB•42's, had more the look of the production B-32.

Fig. 120. The second XB-32 prototype with pressurization and retractable gun turrets.

CONVAIR
B-32 DOMINATOR

Fig. 121. The first production Dominator, a B-32-1-CF.

The production B-32, called Dominator, had many revisions from the experimental craft. Later model Wright R-3350-23 engines turned new four-bladed props with their 2,200 hp. Two exhaust driven supercharges were mounted in each engine nacelle, and inboard propellers could be reversed to shorten the landing roll. A more business-like nose replaced the "greenhouses" of the bombardier and pilots. The new front held a ball type turret at its extreme tip. The bomb aimer's position was just below and behind the turret. Due to a change in operational technique that proved the effectiveness of low altitude bombing, it was considered unnecessary to retain the pressurized cockpit. Elimination of this and the remote gun positions reduced the empty weight to 60,278 pounds and the gross to 100,000 pounds -- a saving of more than two and a quarter tons. The Dominator carried a crew of ten and 8,000 pounds of bombs with 5,460 gallons of fuel.

Further changes provided for two power turrets on top of the fuselage and a retractable turret underneath, armed with twin fifties. A remote tail stinger replaced the manned position on the "X" types. This made a total of ten machine guns with which to defend itself.

An interesting feature of the B-32 was its two sets of landing flaps. Both sets worked independently of each other, which was an advantage in the event of damage or failure.

Only 115 copies of the Convair B-32 were built, and they had a wing span of 135 feet with an area of 1,422 square feet. Length was 82 feet 1 inch; height 32 feet 2 inches. Maximum range was 4,200 miles. Top speed was 357 mph at 30,000 feet and normal cruising speed was 290 mph. Landing speed at a weight of 80,000 pounds was 96 mph.

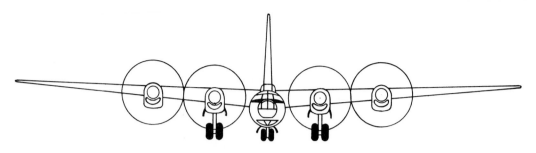

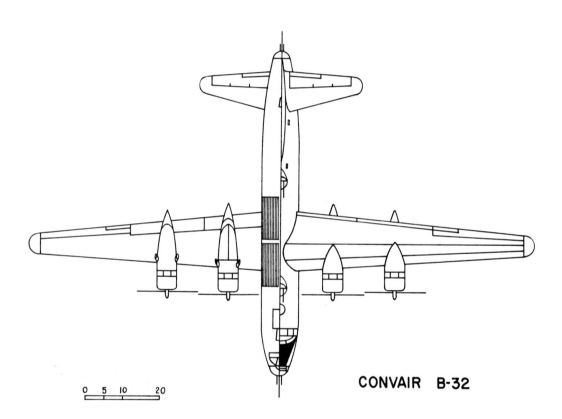

CONVAIR B-32

0 5 10   20

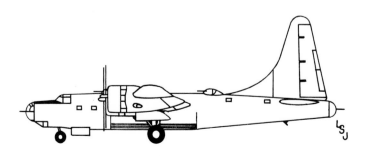

Fig. 122. Convair B-32 Dominator.

Fig. 123. Many of the Dominators were used as trainers. Here is a TB-32-5-CF. Trainer versions carried no armament.

Fig. 124. Another view of the first production B-32 (42-108471).

MARTIN
XB-33

Fig. 125. This photo of the XB-33 model shows the resemblance to Navy PBM series.

While the Army Air Corps was still seeking a high altitude twin engine medium bomber, the Martin Company submitted a design for a pressurized aircraft of this description. Engineering began in October of 1940, and the new ship was to be called the XB-33. It was hoped it would become a replacement for Martin's B-26 Marauder.

As the design took shape on the drawing boards, it started to resemble a very clean, land based variation of a recently developed patrol bomber built by Martin for the U.S. Navy, the PBM Mariner. Two Wright R-3350 eighteen cylinder radial Cyclone engines with 1,800 hp were specified for the ship, which had an approximate wing span of 100 feet. Other

dimensions, also estimated, were a length of 71 feet and height of 22 feet 6 inches.

Continued development of the basic proposal led to an increase in the weight of the airframe. The greater weight made it impossible to achieve the performance requested by the Air Corps with two engines as planned. The bi-motored arrangement was abandoned, and the project was expanded to a four engine machine.

This twin engine design for the XB-33 program is included herein to once again illustrate some of the problems confronting aircraft engineers in their constant effort to improve the performance and safety of American aircraft.

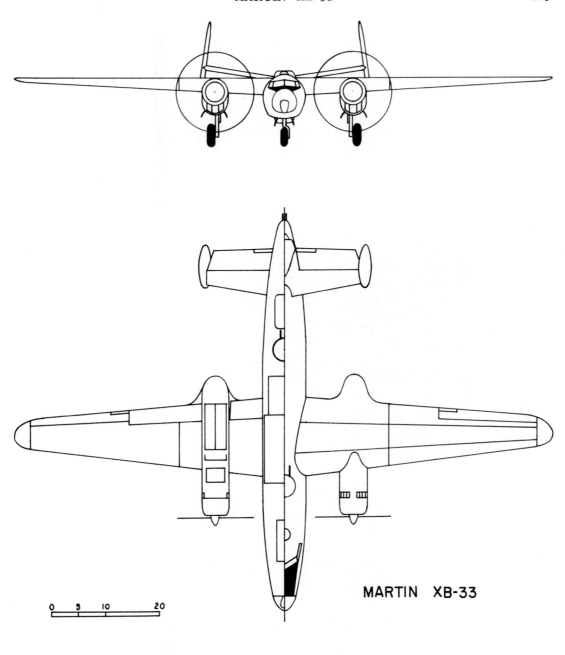

MARTIN XB-33

0 5 10   20

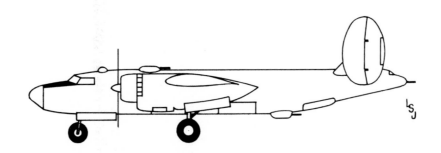

Fig. 126. Martin XB-33 Super Marauder.

Fig. 127. The original proposal for the XB-33 had two engines.

MARTIN
XB-33A SUPER MARAUDER

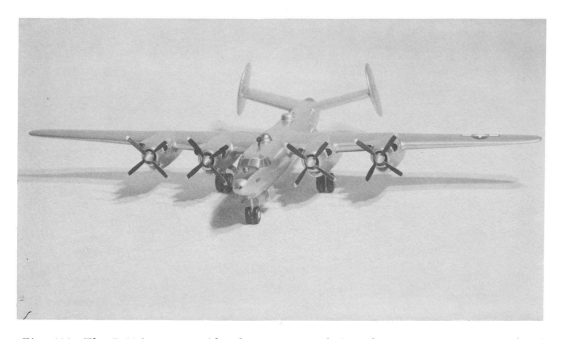

*Fig. 128. The B-33A was considered unnecessary before the prototypes were completed.
Four hundred were cancelled.*

With the conclusion that the original twin engine arrangement of the XB-33 would not be successful, Martin designers suddenly found themselves competing against the Boeing and Convair designs for a large, heavy, four engine aircraft. But the larger XB-33 (Martin Model 190) showed much promise, and Martin was given Contract No. AC-18645 to proceed with construction of two airframes.

Given the apellation Super Marauder, the new XB-33 was to have a 134 foot wing mounting four 1,800 hp Wright R-2600-15 Cyclone 14's. Wing area was 1,500 square feet. The 79 foot 10 inch fuselage incorporated a remote control system for operating the power turrets in the nose, forward belly, upper rear, and tail. An arrangement similar to the B-32 was provided for the bombardier, wherein a notch was cut into the nose below and behind the remote gun position. Total firepower consisted of eight .50 cal. machine guns with 3,000 rounds of am-

munition. Height was 24 feet.

A two stage General Electric CMC-3 turbo supercharger was installed on each engine to enable the plane to reach a service ceiling of 39,000 feet. Rate of climb was figured at 1,135 feet per minute with a maximum range of 2,000 miles at 242 mph. Highest speed attainable was to be 345 mph. Empty weight was 64,948 pounds, gross was 97,917 pounds, and bomb capacity was 10,130 pounds. The fuel tank could hold 4,650 gallons.

The paper performance specifications for the Super Marauder were so encouraging, the Air Corps ordered 400 more of the bombers as the Martin B-33A before the two prototypes were completed. But World War II was in its final stages and there was no longer a need for a third heavy bomber, as even the B-32 was superfluous. As a result, the B-33A production order was cancelled and the incomplete prototypes were dismanteled, thus writing an end to the B-33 project.

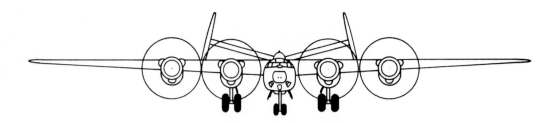

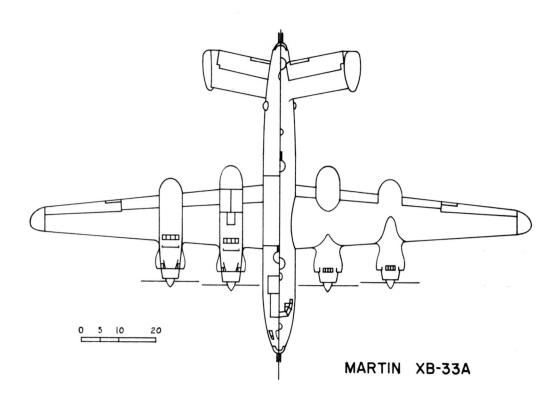

0   5   10   20

MARTIN   XB-33A

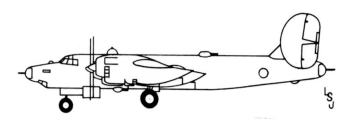

Fig. 129. Martin XB-33A Super Marauder.

Fig. 130. Model shows how four engine B-33A would have appeared.

LOCKHEED - VEGA
B-34 AND B-37 VENTURA

Fig. 131. Lockheed-Vega B-34 Ventura, adapted from the Navy PV-1.

This series of light bombers was an Air Corps version of the Navy PV-1 patrol bomber. The first of 200 B-34 Venturas Vega (Model 137) was accepted in September of 1941 and was given the serial number 41-38020. The design was not spectacularly different in appearance from the types of the day, but it was the first bomber to have all metal control surfaces instead of the metal frame/fabric covering used by its contemporaries. The primary use of the B-34 was in coastal patrols, and for this it was armed with two fixed .50 cal. guns in the nose with two moveable .30's below in the glazed portion. A Martin upper turret held another pair of .50's, and a notch in the lower fuselage provided placement for two more .30's. Six 500 pound bombs could fit into the bomb bay.

The B-34 reached a top speed of 312 mph with its two Pratt & Whitney Double Wasp R-2800-31 engines. Cruising speed was 272 mph, and it could climb at the rate of 2,100 feet per minute. Service ceiling was 25,200 feet, and its 565 gallons of fuel gave it a range of 950 miles. Landing speed was 80 mph.

Weights were lighter than most of the newer twin engine bombers -- 17,233 pounds empty and 26,000 pounds maximum permissable. Gross was 22,500 pounds.

Ventura dimensions remained unaltered throughout its several service versions. These included a wing with a 65 foot 6 inch span and 551 square foot area, 51 foot 5 inch length, and 11 foot 11 inch height.

The B-37 Venturas were converted from a production block of 0-56 reconnaissance planes. As Vega Model 437, they differed from the B-34's in having less powerful R-2600-13 engines by Pratt & Whitney. Highest speed was re-

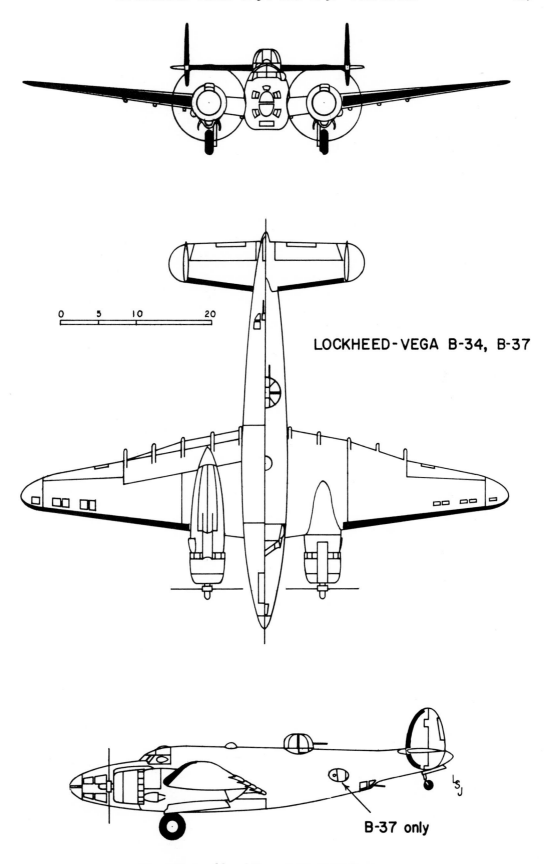

LOCKHEED-VEGA B-34, B-37

B-37 only

Fig. 132. Lockheed-Vega B-34, B-37 Ventura.

Fig. 133. A B-37 Ventura, showing depressed gun position in fuselage side.

duced to 298 mph, and landing speed to 77 mph. Empty weight was 18,615 pounds, and the gross weight remained at 22,500 pounds. The most noticeable difference between the 18 B-37's and the earlier B-34's was the plexiglas depression on the sides to provide a lateral cone of fire for two machine guns.

B-37's had a range of 1,300 miles and a service ceiling of 22,400 feet. Bomb capacity was one ton.

NORTHROP
XB-35 FLYING WING

Fig. 134. The N9M, one of a series of one-third scale models of the XB-35.

On June 25, 1946, American aviation took a bold step into the future. On this date, the world's largest all-wing aircraft triumphantly rose from the runway adjoining the Northrop Aircraft Co. facilities. Here was flying proof that an airplane could perform without the drag-producing fuselage and tail assembly of conventional craft.

This radical concept of aerodynamics was first tested on a series of one-third scale flying models beginning with the N1M in 1940. Designs for the actual bomber were begun in September, 1941, and a contract for one prototype, as the XB-35 (42-13603), followed in November. A second prototype (42-38323) was soon added to the order.

When the completed aircraft made its maiden flight, it was powered by two Pratt & Whitney R-4360-21 Wasp Major engines driving the inboard contra-props

and two R-4360-17's turning the outer pair. Each engine developed 3,000 horsepower. The housing over the prop shafts offered enough area to counteract any yaw tendencies, and the contra-rotating propellers gave additional stability. Cooling air for the radial engines was ducted from openings in the leading edge of the wing.

Control of the plane was achieved by a combination aileron/elevator, or elevon, working in either role as needed. The rudders were comprised of clam shell doors on the trailing edge at the wingtips -- the drag of the open doors producing the necessary yaw. Roll was created by the elevons working in opposition. Automatic slots were located in the leading edge tips. The controls in the cockpit, however, were of the conventional type.

The XB-35 was capable of a maximum speed of 391 mph and a cruising speed of

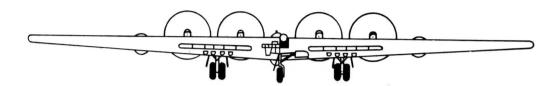

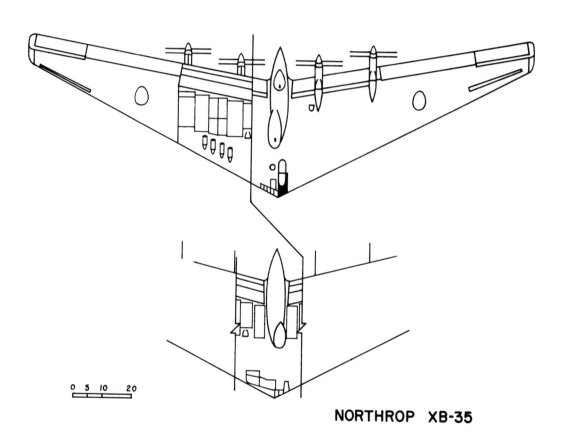

NORTHROP XB-35

0 5 10   20

Fig. 135. Northrop XB-35 Flying Wing.

Fig. 136. The prototype XB-35 presented an awesome spectacle in flight.

183 mph. The wing had a span of 172 feet with a lifting area of 4,000 square feet. Length was 53 feet, and height was 20 feet. The Flying Wing had an empty weight of 89,560 pounds; gross weight was 162,000 pounds, with a maximum capacity for 209,000 pounds. This allowed carrying 41,200 pounds of bombs, and gave a range, with 18,000 gallons of fuel, of 10,000 miles.

A third prototype (42-102366) was completed as the YB-35, and ten more were ordered for further testing. But troubles in the reduction gearing arrangement and propeller governor of the first three proved too great and further development of the B-35 was abandoned.

The armament of the XB-35 was quite formidable. No less than twenty .50 cal. guns were positioned in remote barbettes on the structure. An upper and lower turret on the center section each held four guns. Four more positions above and

Fig. 137. Quite apparent in this view is the unique control system of the Flying Wing.

below the wing, outboard of the engines, each sported two guns. A final cluster of four was located in the "tail" cone. A relief crew of six was carried in addition to the regular operating crew of nine.

For further development of the Flying Wing design, see the Northrop YB-49.

CONVAIR
B-36D

Fig. 138. Convair's huge XB-36 was the first of a series of the largest bombers ever produced.

Certainly the most awe inspiring bomber, if not aircraft in general, was the huge Convair B-36. The descriptive word "giant" can aptly be applied to this ship, the largest airplane ever to reach full production status.

The XB-36 was initially designed in October, 1941, and the Air Corps ordered two test machines a month later. Convair estimated the first plane (42-13570) would be ready for testing in two and a half years, but demands for B-24's and B-32's delayed completion for almost five years. When the enormous craft was finally rolled out, it appeared with a graceful tubular fuselage extending 163 feet and capped by a rudder climbing upward to 46 feet 10 inches. The wing span of 230 feet with an area of 4,772 square feet completed the proportions to make it the largest airplane in the world. And a gross weight of

265,000 pounds made it the heaviest. (Empty weight was 131,740 pounds.)

Integral fuel tanks in the wing spar held 19,976 gallons of fuel for the six Pratt & Whitney R-4360-25 Wasp Major engines, which delivered 3,000 hp to each of the gigantic nineteen foot pusher propellers. As large as the XB-36 was, it possessed a high degree of aerodynamic cleanliness, and following its first flight on August 8, 1946, speeds of 346 mph were reached.

Production B-36A's had a new raised cockpit with a greenhouse type canopy lopping a foot off the fuselage length. Two sets of four-wheel bogie type landing gear replaced the two 9 foot 2 inch tires that had been used on the prototype. The XB-36 was later retrofitted with the four-wheel type gear. Twenty-two B-36A's were completed, and this model could

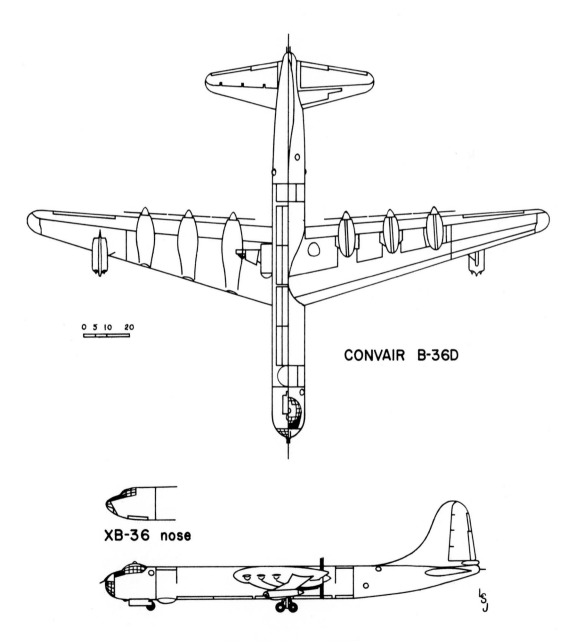

0 5 10 20

CONVAIR B-36D

XB-36 nose

Fig. 139. Convair B-36D.

Fig. 140. *Tremendous size of the B-36A is clearly shown in this view. Serial number is 44-92010.*

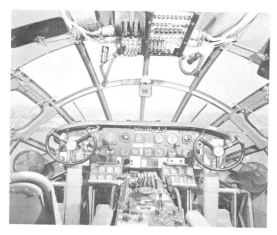

Fig. 141. *Control center of a B-36D. Note jet controls above, piston engine throttles below.*

reach an altitude of 46,100 feet.

An improved B-36B was first flown on July 8, 1948, and was followed by 72 more of the type. These were powered by R-4360-41's with horsepower increased to 3,500. The more powerful engines provided a top speed of 381 mph with a cruise of 202 mph. Landing speed was 115 mph. The B-36B had a service ceiling of 42,000 feet with a rate of climb of 1,510 feet per minute. Extreme range was 10,000 miles. Empty weight was 140,640 pounds; gross was 227,700 pounds.

No B-36C aircraft were built. A description of this radical variation of the B-36 series appears as the next presentation in this history.

Further improvements in performance

of the aerial titan accompanied the addition of four General Electric J-47-GE-19 jet engines giving a boost of 5,200 pounds of thrust each. Aided by six R-4360-41 Wasp Majors, the new model B-36D had a top speed of 439 mph and a service ceiling of 45,200 feet -- quite remarkable for an aircraft of such tremendous proportions. Seventy-one earlier B-36B's were fitted with the jets and otherwise modified to "D" standards. The B-36D had a cruising speed of 225 mph, and could land at 121 mph. Range was 7,500 miles with 10,000 pounds of bombs. A crew of 16 was carried, including 5 relief men. Gross weight was 357,500 pounds, and empty, it weighed 158,843 pounds -- greater than the weight of 17 Keystone XB-1's! Fuel capacity

Fig. 142. *A B-36D and the sole C-99, a cargo development of the huge intercontinental bomber.*

Fig. 143. The XB-36 had fixed slots in the wings. Note number four prop is feathered.

was 32,910 gallons. Rate of climb was 1,740 feet per minute.

This immense bomber carried eight remotely operated turrets, six of which retracted and were covered by faired doors to reduce drag. All guns carried were 20 mm cannons in pairs. Four bays were incorporated for the bomb load. At one time, it was planned to have the B-36 carry its own fighter escort in the form of the McDonnell XF-85 Goblin jet. The little parasite fighter would operate from a trapeze in one of the bomb bays. Folding wings would enable the XF-85 to be carried completely within the fuselage of the larger ship. Although this project was abandoned, a variation was used with the adaptation of a Republic RF-84F and a GRB-36J.

The B-36 crew compartments were

Fig. 144. The NB-36H was used as an atomic reactor test bed. The aircraft was powered by conventional means and the reactor was operated over uninhabited areas.

pressurized, completely airconditioned, and equipped with an oxygen system for use when needed. Forward and aft chambers were connected by a pressurized tunnel running through the bomb compartments. A cart rolling on rails provided transit.

A most unusual variation of the B-36 series was the NB-36H (51-5712) with a nuclear reactor located in the tail for airborne atomic tests. This plane was totally unarmed and had a distinctive cobra-like hood over the cockpit. It was used to determine reaction of nuclear radioactivity on instruments and other operating parts of aircraft in anticipation of atomic powered flight. This plane was not powered by the reactor.

The last of 325 B-36's was retired in May of 1958; the B-36H being the most produced with 154 copies.

Fig. 145. A GRB-36J Ficon carrying an RF-84F.

Fig. 146. A reconnaissance version, RB-36F.

CONVAIR
YB-36C

Fig. 147. The YB-36C with tractor engines did not go beyond the mockup stage.

The YB-36C was a proposed attempt to improve the performance of the B-36 type bomber with the installation of six 4,300 horsepower Pratt & Whitney R-4360-51 VDT engines. With power supplied by the VDT (Variable Discharge Turbine) engine, it was hoped to increase the speed of the aircraft to 410 mph.

The R-4360-51 engine had water injection for take-off with fuel injection to each of the 27 cylinders. Exhaust gasses passed through the turbine of a G. E. CHM-2 turbosupercharger at all times. A clamshell nozzle controlled the power by varying the size of the turbine exit. This was operated by an automatic control activated by a manifold pressure sensing device.

In order to utilize the additional power from the turbine nozzle, the conventional rearward facing of the B-36 engine was reversed. Since the new engine was to occupy the same position aft of the rear main spar as the standard B-36, it was

necessary to extend the prop shaft forward out the leading edge of the wing. The reduction gear was in the nose of the rigidly mounted boom which extended about ten feet forward of the wing. Four vibration shock mounts held the boom in place.

Cooling air was ducted through inlets beside the nacelle extension and across the face of the engine. A two-speed fan drew the air past the engine and exhausted it through cowl flaps in the rear part of the nacelle.

The Pratt & Whitney Division of United Aircraft gives these specifications for this engine:

"The proposed R-4360-51 engine was rated as follows:

Takeoff	4300 SHP @ 2800 RPM		wet
	4000	2800	dry
Military	4300	2800	wet
	4000	2800	dry
Normal	3100	2600	dry"

Although the project was approved in

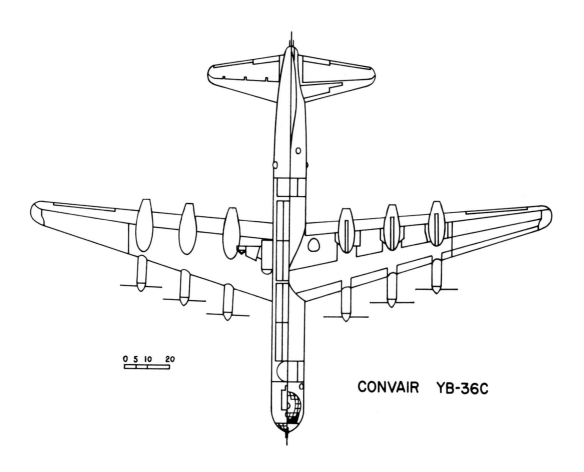

0 5 10 20

CONVAIR YB-36C

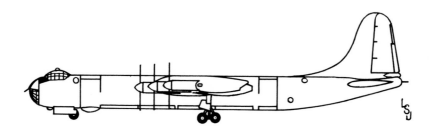

Fig. 148. Convair YB-36C.

Fig. 149. Photo of the model shows modified engine nacelles for the VDT engines. This plane was completed as a B-36B.

October, 1947, the engine did not materialize, so on May 21, 1948, the YB-36C designation was cancelled and the 34 planes destined for the tractor installation were completed as B-36B's. Dimensions of the YB-36C were a wing span of 230 feet, wing area of 4,772 square feet, length of 162 feet, height of 46 feet 10 inches.

LOCKHEED - VEGA
XB-38 FLYING FORTRESS

Fig. 150. The XB-38 offered improved performance over the B-17E.

In March, 1942, the Vega subsidiary of Lockheed Aircraft suggested the installation of Allison V-1710-89 liquid cooled engines to step up the performance of the B-17. On July 10, 1942, the Air Corps awarded them contract number AC-28120 to modify one airframe to mount these powerplants. For this purpose, the ninth production Boeing B-17E (41-2401) was selected and given the new designation Vega XB-38. On May 19, 1943, the 12 cylinder, 1,425 horsepower engines lifted the ship on its first flight, and the following tests showed a top speed of 327 mph -- an improvement of 10 mph over the production B-17E. In addition to the inline engines, the XB-38 featured new wingtip fuel tanks, which increased the capacity by 1,080 gallons to a new quantity of 2,810 gallons normally carried and extended the range to 3,600 miles. Full-feathering hydromatic propellers were also installed.

This version of the Flying Fortress weighed 34,748 pounds empty and had a maximum gross of 64,000 pounds. Heaviest bomb capacity was 6,000 pounds with a range of 1,900 miles thus loaded. Service ceiling was 29,700 feet, and cruising speed was 226 mph. Armament remained the same as the basic B-17E series.

While flight tests showed considerable promise with the Allison engines, an in-flight fire in one of the installations led to the destruction of the aircraft on June 16, 1943, just 29 days after its maiden flight. Due to the need of the Allison engines for other aircraft in production, further development was halted.

The XB-38 had a wing span of 103 feet 9 inches, length of 74 feet, and height of 19 feet 2 inches. Wing area was 1,420 square feet.

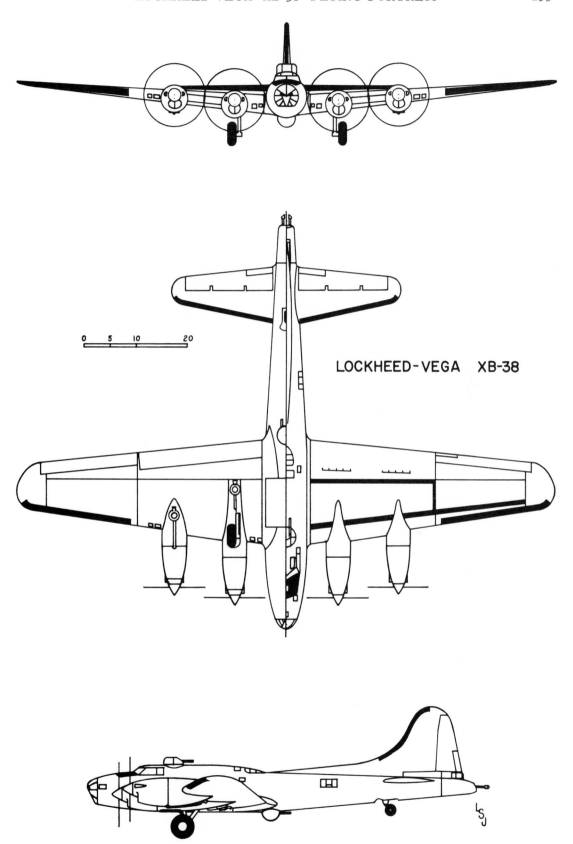

LOCKHEED-VEGA XB-38

Fig. 151. Lockheed-Vega XB-38 Flying Fortress.

Fig. 152. Additional air intakes for the Allison engines were located between the nacelles.

BOEING
XB-39 SPIRIT OF LINCOLN

Fig. 153. The XB-39 test vehicle was converted from the first YB-29.

In a development program comparable to that undertaken by Vega on the XB-38, Boeing placed their first YB-29 at the disposal of General Motors for flight tests with the 24 cylinder Allison V-3420-11. This engine was first ordered in 1937 for testing by the Air Corps, and is unique in possessing two crankshafts which turn over the single prop hub. Essentially, the V-3420 engine is made up of two V-1710's with a common crankcase. This gives a frontal appearance similar to the letter "W". Most of the parts of the V-3420 are interchangeable with the V-1710 series. The engines used on the XB-39 were rated at 3,000 horsepower.

With the boost in power, the XB-39 showed a top speed of 405 mph at an altitude of 25,000 feet. Its cruising speed was 282 mph. Service ceiling was 35,000 feet; and with an initial rate of climb of 1,300 feet per minute, 30,000 feet could be reached in 29.3 minutes. Its maximum range was 6,290 miles with 3,333 gallons of fuel. An empty weight of 75,037 pounds was 3 tons more than the B-29B, but the gross weight of 105,000 pounds was much lighter than the parent series.

Only one XB-39 was converted, but the results of the testing proved conclusively that the additional power improved performance without undue side effects.

The basic dimensions of this conversion remained the same as the YB-29: span, 141 feet 3 inches; length, 99 feet; height, 29 feet 7 inches; wing area, 1,728 square feet. The crew varied from six to twelve men.

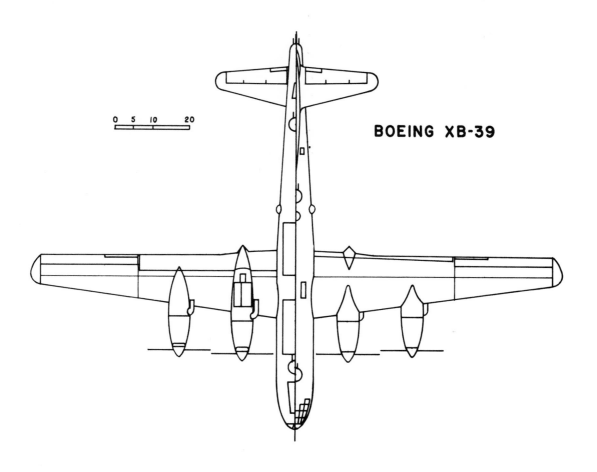

BOEING XB-39

0 5 10   20

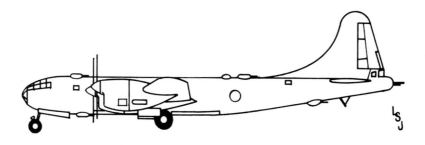

Fig. 154. Boeing XB-39 Spirit of Lincoln.

Fig. 155. This B-29 modification was virtually powered by eight engines.

LOCKHEED - VEGA
YB-40 FLYING FORTRESS

Fig. 156. One of the thirteen YB-40 escort Fortresses.

One of the major problems confronting Allied bomber groups during the Second World War was the lack of fighter protection on long range missions. The proportions of a bomber were ideal for a large fuel capacity, but the trim lines and light weight necessitated by the performance requirements of a fighter made long range escort missions impractical.

In August of 1942, a program for a veritable "flying destroyer" was begun. The Vega Aircraft Co. took the second Boeing B-17F (41-24341) and began rebuilding it as the XB-40. Although it was no longer a bomber, it did bear the "B" designation. The prototype was completed in four months. For its new role, the airplane had been fitted with a Bendix chin turret -- of the type to be later adopted

for the B-17G's -- and an additional Martin upper turret at the rear of the dorsal cockpit fairing. A new streamlined plexiglas nose was installed, behind which sat the chin turret operator. There were seven pairs of .50 calibre machine guns supplied with 5,900 rounds of ammunition. A further 6,500 rounds were held in reserve. Supply tracks led to the waist and tail gunners for a speedy replenishment when the ammunition ran low.

Thirteen more B-17F's were converted to YB-40's, and these differed from the "X" mainly in having the cockpit fairing cut short of the mid-dorsal position. This allowed a better coverage for the turret.

The service record of the B-40's was a disappointment, as they proved too heavy and even had difficulties defending themselves from fighter assaults. The

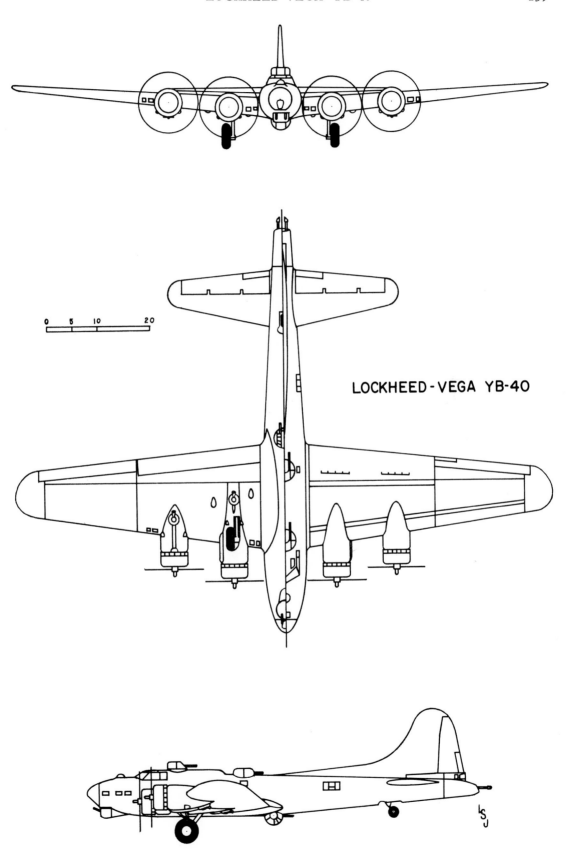

LOCKHEED-VEGA YB-40

Fig. 157. Lockheed-Vega YB-40 Flying Fortress.

Fig. 158. Dark spots of paint show where the modifications were undertaken on the XB-40.

additional armor made the B-40 tail heavy and keeping formation with bombers was difficult. But even worse, was the fact that the heavier escort plane could not keep up with the bombers after their load had been dropped, and to add to their embarrassment, the escorts had to be escorted home! Needless to say, the whole idea was soon abandoned and the YB-40's were either reconverted to bombers or used as trainers.

This variation of the Flying Fortress had four Wright R-1820-97 Cyclone engines of 1,200 hp. Empty weight was 38,235 pounds and gross was 58,000 pounds. Maximum weight was 63,500 pounds and included a reported 40,000 rounds of ammunition. Top speed was 292 mph, landing at 94 mph. Eight of the crew of ten acted as gunners. Extreme range was 2,460 miles with a service ceiling of 29,200 feet. Wing span was 103 feet 9 inches, area 1,420 square feet, length was 74 feet 9 inches, and height was 19 feet 1 inch.

Fig. 159. The XB-40 was distinguished by the cockpit fairing extending to the second dorsal turret and a small blister at the waist window.

CONVAIR
XB-41 LIBERATOR

Fig. 160. A Convair B-24D as the XB-41 escort Liberator. Front Martin turret is raised in this view, was later lowered to standard position.

The attempt to develop an escort version of the B-24 met with even less success than the ill-fated YB-40. At the same time the B-17 experiment was authorized, work began on a Convair B-24D -- serial number 41-11822 -- to provide fighter protection for bomber formations. Testing of the airplane took place between February 2, and February 13, 1943.

As the XB-41, the Liberator armament was boosted by the incorporation of a Bendix chin turret, a Motor Products tail turret, and a second Martin power turret amidship. To avoid restricting the line of fire due to the second turret location, the front turret was raised from its original position. This proved unnecessary and was later returned to its former arrangement. Unusual was the fact that the left waist position was occupied by a powered turret while the right side had an open hatch. The turret blister was a cause of complaint due to the excess wind it allowed to enter the fuselage.

Among other adverse features found during the testing was the hydraulic system for firing the waist guns. The system was such that operation of the guns on one side interfered with the other pair. On one test, the trigger mechanism failed, causing one of the guns to run away. In other tests, the tail guns continued firing after the gunner had released the foot trigger; and it was generally agreed by all the gunners involved, that the tail turret doors should not come open during firing!

But in spite of the difficulties encountered, the tests proved generally successful and a recommendation was made to include the design features on B-24 type airplanes intended for use as special convoy fighters. However, the installations affected the stability of the XB-41, and no further modifications or testing were undertaken.

The XB-41 had fourteen .50 cal.

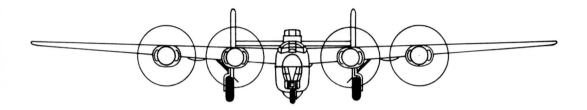

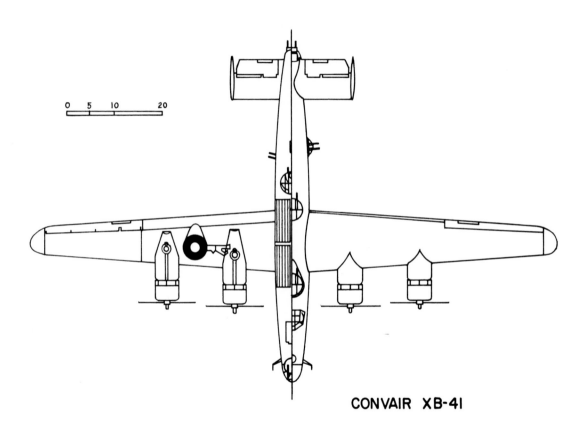

0   5   10   20

CONVAIR XB-41

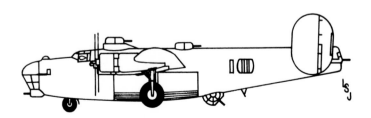

Fig. 161. Convair XB-41 Liberator.

Fig. 162. XB-41 was "paper" designation of B-24D No. 41-11822.

machine guns paired in the seven defensive positions. A reserve of 4,100 rounds of ammunition was carried in a box attached in the forward bomb bay. The maximum ammunition capacity amounted to 12,420 rounds.

Power and dimensions of the XB-41 were the same as the B-24D: 4 Pratt & Whitney R-1830-43 Twin Wasps of 1,250 hp; span 110 feet; length 66 feet 4 inches; height 17 feet 11 inches. Due to the additional armor and armament, the XB-41 weighed slightly more, however. Empty, it was 37,050 pounds, and gross 63,000 pounds. Top speed was 289 mph, with a service ceiling of 28,500 feet. Range as an escort was 3,100 miles.

Fig. 163. Bendix chin turret installation on XB-41.

Fig. 164. A powered waist turret was used on the port side. Starboard side had conventional hatch.

DOUGLAS
XB-42 MIXMASTER

Fig. 165. The prototype Mixmaster, XB-42. Note the unusual mounting of the guns in the trailing edge of the wing.

Douglas' radical new attack bomber, the XA-42, was in the development stages early in 1943, when the Air Corps saw in it a potential inexpensive substitute for the Boeing B-29. Redesignating it into the bomber classification as the XB-42, (the 42nd bomber and attack designs happened to coincide) a contract was awarded in August, 1943.

The first XB-42 (serial number 43-50225) -- dubbed Mixmaster because of the churning effect of the dual pusher props -- was flown on May 6, 1944. As a long range bomber, it could fly 5,400 miles and had a capacity for 8,000 pounds of destruction in its bomb bay. With the bomb doors open five inches, a single 10,000 pound bomb could be carried. A top speed in excess of 450 mph made it the fastest American bomber yet seen. On one flight, the XB-42 set a transcontinental speed record with an average speed of 433 mph.

The two 1,800 hp Allison V-1710-125

engines were mounted beside each other behind the cockpit; their power reaching the contra-rotating propellers via two sets of five P-39 drive shafts. Radiator cooling air entered ducts in the wing root. Both a conventional one piece cockpit and the twin bubble type were tried on the prototypes. Crew was three men.

A second copy was built as the XB-42A (43-50224) and mounted two Westinghouse 19B-2 jet engines under the wings. These gave an additional push of 1,600 pounds of thrust each and a top speed of 488 mph.

An unusual arrangement of armament placed two pairs of .50 cal. machine guns in the trailing edge of the wings between the ailerons and flaps. Aiming and firing was done by the co-pilot who would face rearward for this operation. Two more .50's were fixed to fire forward.

With the war drawing to an end, there was no need for production of these ships, and the original two examples were the

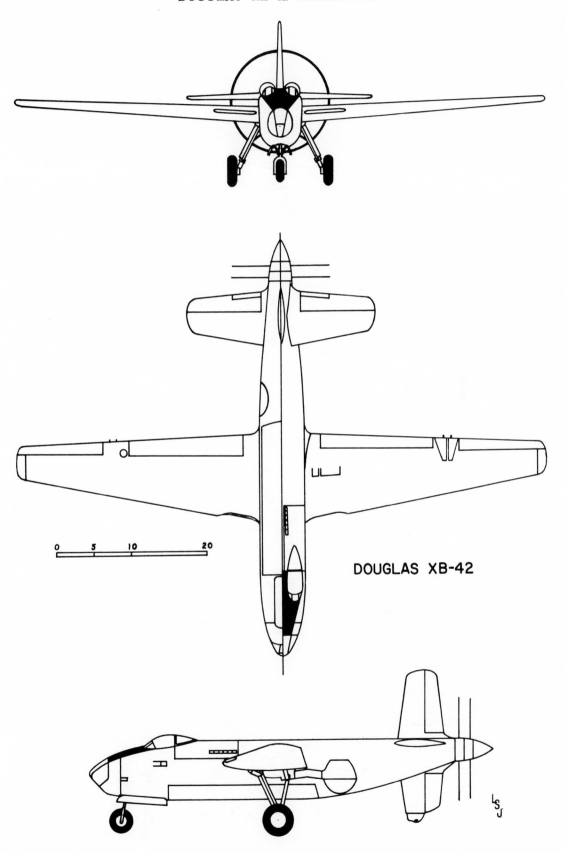

DOUGLAS XB-42

Fig. 166. Douglas XB-42 Mixmaster.

Fig. 167. The XB-42A, second of the type, before mounting the two Westinghouse jet engines.

only ones built. Both eventually crashed.

The XB-42 had a service ceiling of 29,400 feet, an empty weight of 20,888 pounds, a gross weight of 33,200 pounds, and a fuel capacity of 1,750 gallons. The uncluttered wing had a span of 70 feet 6 inches and an area of 555 square feet. The fuselage was 53 feet 7 inches long,

and the rudder was 20 feet 10 inches high.

The following pertains to the XB-42 A: Empty weight, 24,775 pounds; gross weight, 39,000 pounds; fuel capacity, 2,402 gallons; cruising speed, 250 mph; range 4,750 miles.

Fig. 168. A total of ten Airacobra prop shafts drove the two contra props on the Mixmaster.

DOUGLAS
XB-43

Fig. 169. The XB-43 was the first American jet bomber.

The first American bomber to be powered by jet propulsion alone first flew on May 17, 1946. It was a direct descendant of the prop driven XB-42 and bore the next number in the bomber series. While the XB-43 showed a strong resemblance to its immediate ancestor, the modifications were extensive. Two General Electric J35-GE-3 engines with 4,000 pounds of thrust were encased in the fuselage. Thus powered, the XB-43 reached 507 mph and led the way into a new realm of speed for such aircraft. Under certain conditions, however, the plane showed instability, and with newer bombers in the development stages, it was not considered suitable for production.

A second prototype was completed and, as the YB-43 (44-61509), was put to work in an extensive engine testing program. Though originally powered by the J35's, one of these engines was replaced by the engine involved in the evaluation. A change in performance did not adversely affect the trim of the YB-43 as the engines were mounted so close to the airplane centerline.

Both airframes were provided with bomb bays, but no bomb racks were installed. An 8,000 pound bomb load was proposed, and range as a bomber would have been 2,500 miles at 420 mph. The XB-43 had an empty weight of 22,890 pounds and grossed 40,000 pounds. Service ceiling was 38,500 feet, and the rate of climb was 2,470 feet per minute. Performance and weights given are for the XB-43, as the characteristics of the YB-43 with a test engine would vary considerably and be misleading. Dimensions were the same, however, with a span of 71 feet 2 inches, a length of 51 feet 5 inches, and a height of 24 feet 3 inches. The wing had an area of 563 square feet. The fuel tanks held 2,309 gallons.

The XB-43 now forms a part of the National Aeronautical Collection at the Smithsonian Institution in Washington, D. C. The YB-43 was eventually retired from service.

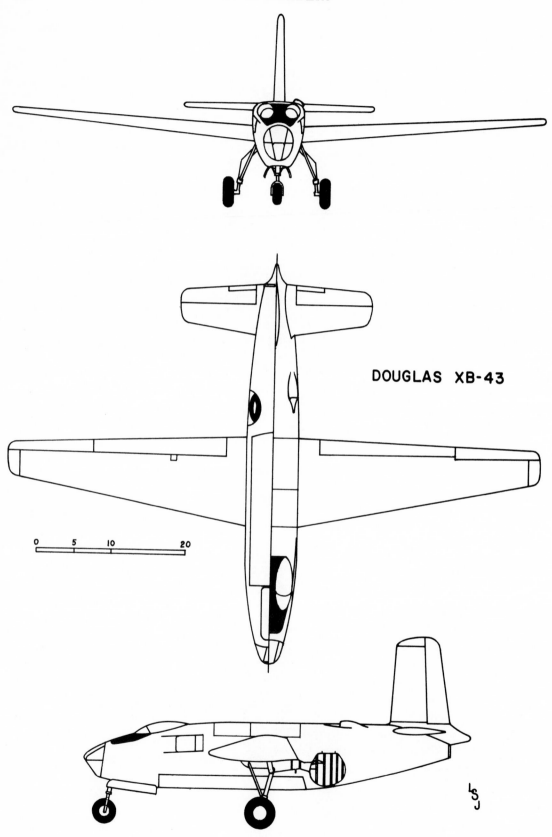

Fig. 170. Douglas XB-43.

Fig. 171. The YB-43 was nicknamed "Versatile II" due to it's adaptability as an engine test bed.

PRATT & WHITNEY
XB-44 SUPERFORTRESS

Fig. 172. The XB-44 was converted by Pratt & Whitney to utilize the new Wasp Major engines.

In September, 1943, the Pratt & Whitney engine company offered a plan to boost the performance of the B-29 by replacing the Wright R-3350's with larger Pratt & Whitney R-4360-33 Wasp Major's of 3,000 horsepower. In July of the following year, a contract was awarded for the altering of one B-29 airframe for this purpose.

The R-4360 engines, being bulkier than the Wright's, required a complete redesign of the nacelles and part of the wing. The results of these changes was given the designation XB-44, and had a serial number 42-93845. The ship first took to the air in May, 1945, and showed a top speed of 392 mph. However, since the plane was to be used exclusively for engine testing, all but two .50 cal. guns in the tail had been removed, making the gross weight only 105,000 pounds. Empty weight was 75,035 pounds. Maxi-

mum fuel capacity was 9,300 gallons, which gave the engines enough gas for a range of 2,400 miles, cruising at 282 mph.

Gear driven superchargers were installed on the engines to help obtain a service ceiling of 29,000 feet. At gross weight, the XB-44 could climb to 30,000 in 35 minutes.

Results of the XB-44 testing led to the development of the B-50 series of Superfortresses, described later in this book. Although many test vehicles do not progress beyond the experimental stage, the XB-44 is an example of how such aircraft can lead to a vastly improved product from a basic design.

XB-44 dimensions were a wing span of 141 feet 3 inches, a wing area of 1,728 square feet, a length of 99 feet, and a height of 29 feet 7 inches.

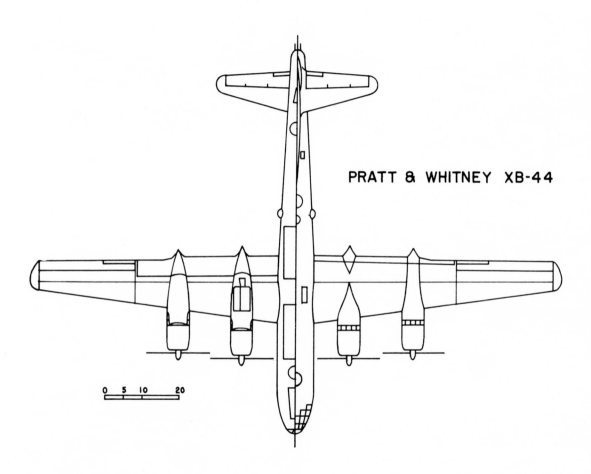

PRATT & WHITNEY XB-44

0   5   10   20

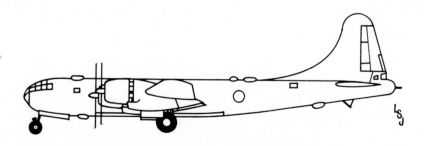

Fig. 173. Pratt & Whitney XB-44 Superfortress.

Fig. 174. The airframe which became the XB-44 was the 2nd B-29A-5-BN.

NORTH AMERICAN
B-45 TORNADO

Fig. 175. This B-45C is shown in the role of engine test bed.

That the jet age had begun making inroads in bomber design was apparent with the appearance of the Douglas XB-43 test aircraft. In mid 1944, the Air Force requested bids for a high performance, all jet design. North American showed their proposed model NA-130 and received a contract for three planes as the XB-45 (45-59479 to 45-59481). On March 17, 1947, the XB-45 became the first four jet American bomber to fly.

Power came from four Allison J35-A-4 engines of 4,000 pounds of thrust each, mounted in pairs beneath the wings. The ninety-six B-45A's that followed had more powerful General Electric J47-GE-9 engines with 5,200 pounds of thrust.

These gave a top speed of 580 mph to the Tornado. This model had a climb rate of 6,900 feet per minute and a service ceiling of 46,250 feet. It tipped the scales at 45,206 pounds unloaded and 81,418 pounds gross. Jet fuel carried came to 5,746 gallons to provide for a range of 2,234 miles maximum. For a short distance, 22,000 pounds of bombs could be carried. Cruising speed was 458 mph, landing at 123 mph.

The B-45B was an unbuilt version with a radar fire control system. The B-45C and RB-45C were the next production type with 10 and 33 being the respective quantities built. These were powered by a 5,200 pound thrust J47-

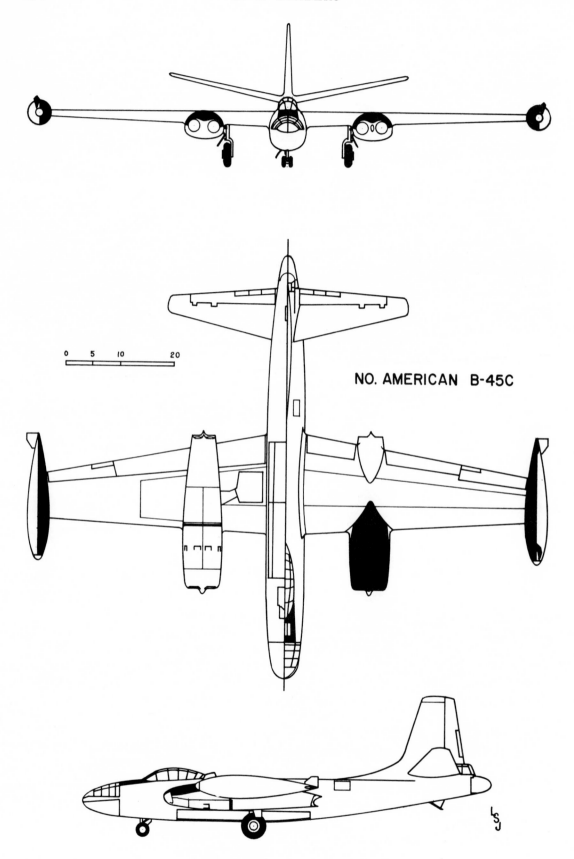

NO. AMERICAN B-45C

Fig. 176. North American B-45C Tornado.

Fig. 177. An RB-45C photo reconnaissance bomber. Transparent nose was replaced by a solid camera bay.

GE-13 and a 6,000 pound wet J47-GE-15 in each nacelle. Top speed was 579 mph. The RB-45C held five camera positions in the nose for photo reconnaissance work.

All versions of the B-45 were armed only with two tail mounted .50 cal. machine guns, and a crew of four was carried.

Statistics for the B-45C show an empty weight of 48,903 pounds with a gross of 82,600 pounds. Additional fuel was carried in wingtip tanks bringing the capacity to 7,996 gallons and extending the range to 2,610 miles. Up to 22,000 pounds of bombs could be carried. Rate of climb was 5,800 feet per minute, and the service ceiling was 43,200 feet. The 45C landed at 141 mph. Wing span was 96 feet with the tanks; area, without tanks, was 1,175 square feet. Length was 75 feet 4 inches, and overall height reached 25 feet 2 inches.

CONVAIR
XB-46

Fig. 178. The Convair XB-46 was one of the cleanest bombers to fly but was not sufficiently advanced to merit production.

For the 1944 jet bomber competition, Convair offered their graceful Model 109, to be powered by four General Electric J35-C-3 engines of 4,000 pounds thrust. The original contract called for three examples to be built as the XB-46, but funds for two of these were later diverted to the Convair XB-53 program, to be discussed later.

The single aircraft built was ready for its first flight on April 2, 1947. (Serial number 45-59582.) The slim exterior belied its 48,018 pounds empty weight and 91,000 pound gross. The extremely thin wings had a span of 113 feet with an area of 1,285 square feet. The oval fuselage, with a bomb capacity of up to 22,000 pounds, stretched to 105 feet 9 inches. Height was 27 feet 11 inches.

On a flight to Wright Field, the XB-46 averaged 533 mph. Highest speed attainable was 545 mph at 15,000 feet. Cruising speed was 439 mph, and service ceiling was 43,000 feet. Six thousand, six hundred eighty-two gallons of fuel could be carried.

Landing gear was pneumatically activated, and the Fowler flaps were lowered by electric motors. The proposed armament was two .50 cal. machine guns mounted in the tail cone with 600 rounds of ammunition each. These were to be aimed and fired by radar. The crew was comprised of the pilot, co-pilot, and bombardier/navigator.

No production orders for the XB-46 were issued, as the design had been made obsolete by the new Boeing XB-47.

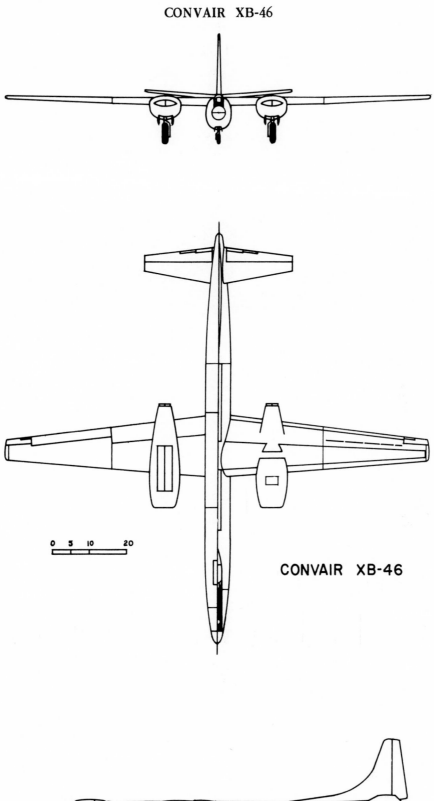

0 5 10 20

CONVAIR XB-46

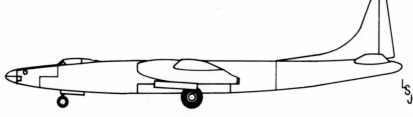

Fig. 179. Convair XB-46.

Fig. 180. The slim fuselage housed a three man crew and 22,000 pounds of bombs.

Fig. 181. Although the XB-46 was classed as a medium bomber, it was larger than some of the World War II heavy bombers.

BOEING
B-47E STRATOJET

Fig. 182. The first Boeing XB-47 prototype.

The third aircraft company to be awarded a development contract in the 1944 Air Force competition was Boeing with a straight wing design, which housed the four jet engines in the fuselage. This configuration was given the original XB-47 label. Results of preliminary testing did not encourage this type of arrangement, however. Tests continued on various designs with none offering the advanced performance sought.

In September, 1945, a swept back wing was introduced as a result of reports studied in Germany after the war. This was what had been needed. The next problem was the engine location. More

than fifty different positions and combinations were tried before the final placing was decided. This became Boeing Model 450, or B-47.

The arrowlike shape of the XB-47 introduced a new look into the field of heavy, high performance aircraft. On December 17, 1947, the swept wing bomber lifted from the runway on its first flight.

The testing that followed proved the soundness of the radical design, and production contracts were awarded that eventually made the Stratojet the backbone of the Strategic Air Command. Ten B-47A's made up the original order and

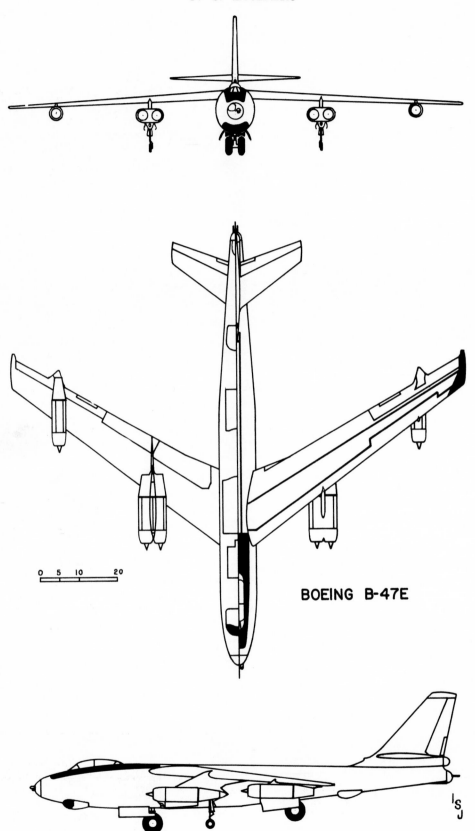

0 5 10   20

BOEING B-47E

Fig. 183. Boeing B-47E Stratojet.

Fig. 184. B-47 Stratojet. Note absence of insignia and markings on undersides. White paint is used to reflect heat from nuclear explosions.

were followed by 398 B-47B aircraft. These two types were powered by six General Electric J47-GE-11 and -23 engines which gave up to 5,800 pounds of thrust -- 1,800 pounds more than the prototype's J35-GE-7 units. Top speed of these types were well over 600 mph with a bombing capability extending over 3,000 miles.

The B-47C was also known as the XB-56 and is covered separately in this book. Two B-47 aircraft were modified to XB-47D's in 1955 when the inboard engine pods were replaced by Curtiss-Wright YT49-W-1 turboprop engines of 10,000 horsepower.

The first B-47E was flown on January 30, 1953. This version is powered by six J47-GE-25A jets with 6,000 pounds of thrust, or 7,200 pounds wet. Two

radar directed 20 mm cannon were mounted in the tail cone as sole defense since the speed of modern jet bombers makes conventional forward armament useless. Maximum bomb capacity is 20,000 pounds with a range of 1,600 miles, which can be extended by inflight refueling. Top speed is Mach 0.65, or 630 mph, at 10,000 feet, cruising at 495 mph. Empty weight is approximately 80,000 pounds and normal loaded weight is 175,000 pounds. Fuel capacity exceeds 17,000 gallons. Dimensions are typical of the series; span, 116 feet; length, 109 feet 10 inches; height, 27 feet 11 inches; wing area, 1,428 square feet.

The Stratojet was the first production bomber to utilize the unique "bicycle" type landing gear, although not the first aircraft to be so equipped.

Fig. 185. A B-47E shows the flexible swept wing. The thin structure flexes several feet at the tips.

Other variations of the B-47 include the reconnaissance and weather-photo types as the RB-47E and RB-47K. The ERB-47H is a radar loaded Stratojet which carries a crew of five instead of the normal three.

As B-47's are being phased out of active service, many of them are being converted to QB-47 radio-control drones for use in missile evaluation tests.

Fig. 186. The XB-47D was used to evaluate high speed turboprop aircraft.

Fig. 187. An ERB-47H points its radar packed nose at the camera.

MARTIN
XB-48

Fig. 188. The bulky XB-48 was a transition into the jet era.

Another six engine jet bomber was ordered for the 1944 evaluation competition, and this one appeared in the form of the Martin Model 223, or XB-48.

The six Allison-built General Electric J35-A-5 engines were encased in individual nacelles in two clusters under the wing. Sheet metal joined the area beneath the engines and formed two tunnels between the nacelles for a cooling air passage. As a result, these shrouds gave the appearance of two huge engine pods. The first of the two XB-48's flew on June 22, 1947, (serial number 45-59585) and the 4,000 pound thrust of each engine provided enough push to reach a top speed of 495 mph.

As in the other designs of the competition, the bomb bay had the ability to encase one 20,000 pound bomb for a short haul. Normal distance flown was 2,500 miles leaving 8,000 pounds of destruction before returning home. The XB-48's service ceiling was 43,000 feet with a rate of climb of 2,600 feet per minute. Empty weight was 58,260 pounds, and gross weight came up to 102,600 pounds, including 4,968 gallons of fuel. The 1,330 square foot wing spanned 108 feet 4 inches; overall length of the aircraft was 85 feet 8 inches, and the height was 26 feet 6 inches.

The XB-48 was the first aircraft designed for the new "bicycle" type landing gear. This feature was necessitated by the use of wings which were too thin to house conventional landing gear with its bulky retracting mechanisms. With the greatest portion of the weight supported by main wheels in the fuselage, small outriggers were used to balance the airplane.

The planes carried a crew of three, and although no guns were installed, it was planned to use two radar directed .50's in the tail.

The flight testing of the XB-48's did not show enough advancement of performance to merit a production order.

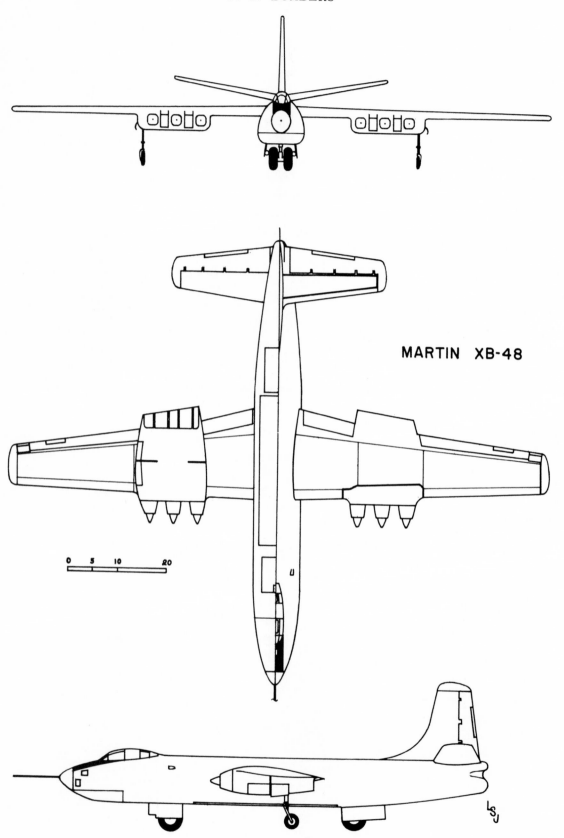

MARTIN XB-48

Fig. 189. Martin XB-48.

Fig. 190. Martin's XB-48 helped pioneer the bicycle type landing gear for heavy bombers.

NORTHROP
YB-49 AND YRB-49A FLYING WING

Fig. 191. The first all jet Flying Wing bomber, powered by eight J35 engines.

Since most of the difficulties encountered in the XB-35 were restricted to the engines and propellers, it was hoped to develop the design into a successful platform by using all jet power. A contract ordering the conversion of two of the Wings was issued on June 1, 1945. This specified installation of eight Allison J35-A-5 engines of 4,000 pounds of thrust, and the aircraft designation became YB-49.

The eight jet version of the Flying Wing weighed 88,100 pounds when it was rolled out. The normal loaded weight was 205,000 pounds, but this could be boosted to 213,000 pounds. On October 21, 1947, the first pure jet Wing was flown (serial number 42-102367). Subsequent flight tests pushed the plane to a top speed of

520 mph and placed the service ceiling at 42,000 feet. A fuel capacity of 17,545 gallons permitted a range of 4,450 miles. The YB-49 was capable of carrying 36,760 pounds of bombs for a distance of 1,150 miles.

After twenty months of testing, during which payload and endurance records were broken, the first YB-49 disintegrated in flight. Nine months later, the second plane was destroyed during landing. However, development had continued on a six jet reconnaissance version known as the YRB-49A. The clean lines of the YB-49 were broken by two engine pods suspended below the four buried jets. Six 5,000 pound thrust Allison J35-A-19's were used. This ship first took to the air on May 4, 1950, and weighed 88,500

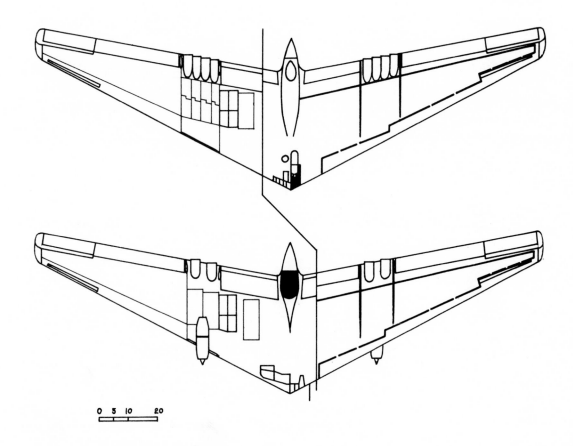

NORTHROP YB-49
& YRB-49A

Fig. 192. Northrop YB-49 & YRB-49A Flying Wing.

Fig. 193. The YRB-49A, a photo reconnaissance version of the Flying Wing, taking off from the Northrop field.

fins protruded from the surface to replace the yaw-dampening prop shaft housings on the earlier type. No armament was installed on the YB-49's, but provision was made for four tail cone mounted .50 cal. machine guns. The YB-49 carried a crew of seven, while the YRB-49A was manned by only five.

The Wing had a span of 172 feet, a length of 53 feet 1 inch, and stood 20 feet high. Wing area was 4,000 square feet.

pounds empty with overload capacity reaching 206,000 pounds, carrying 15,231 gallons of fuel. After a short period of testing this plane, the entire Flying Wing project was abandoned.

The means of controlling the jet version of the Wing was similar to that used by the XB-35. However, four stubby

As an airplane, the Flying Wing was a success, but it has been said that such an advanced design concept was almost 20 years ahead of its time. Even now, all-wing aircraft are reappearing on engineers drawing boards, and the time may soon arrive when this will be the symbol of flight.

Fig. 194. The YRB-49A was the only Flying Wing to have full tactical equipment, and was the last of the series.

BOEING
B-50D SUPERFORTRESS

Fig. 195. Boeing's B-50D, a much cleaner development of the original Superfortress.

The last propeller driven bomber type to be delivered to the U. S. Air Force was the Boeing B-50. This ship was first identified as the B-29D, but the modifications incorporated in the design left only 25 per cent of the original structure, hence, the new designation.

The result of tests on the XB-44 led to the installation of the Pratt & Whitney R-4360-35 Wasp Major engines rated at 3,500 horsepower. The new rudder had been increased in height to 32 feet 8 inches and could be lowered to one side to permit using existing hangars. The 141 foot 3 inch wing span, 99 foot length, and 1,720 square foot wing area were the same as on the earlier B-29's.

The first of the type to fly was a production B-50A, and the event occurred on June 25, 1947. A total of 79 of this model were completed. Top speed was 385 mph, cruising at 235 mph. Touchdown speed was 136 mph.

The B-50 carved its niche in the annals of history on March 2, 1949. A B-50A, serial number 46-010, with the nickname "Lucky Lady II", became the first airplane to fly nonstop around the world. The 23,452 mile flight was made with the aid of aerial tankers which refueled the plane four times using the Probe and Drogue system. This plane was later given to the Smithsonian Institution for preservation.

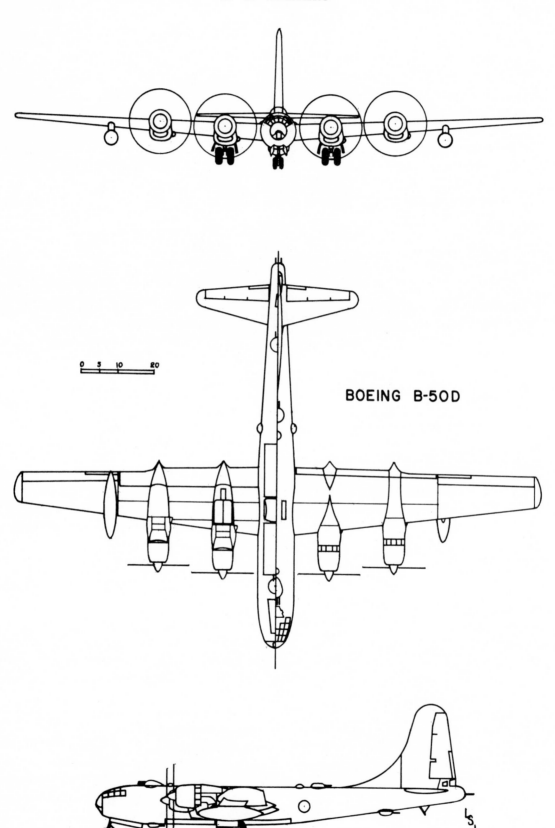

0 5 10   20

BOEING B-50D

Fig. 196. Boeing B-50D Superfortress.

Fig. 197. External 700 gallon fuel tanks were standard on the B-50D.

The next production run turned out 45 B-50B's. These were followed by 222 B-50D's which had a new four gun upper turret -- making a total of 13 .50's --, a solid plexiglas nose instead of the earlier segmented type, and two 700 gallon external fuel tanks. Each tank pylon could be adapted to carry a 4,000 pound bomb. In this new form, the B-50 weighed 80,609 pounds empty, 173,000 full, and carried 11,685 gallons of fuel. In-flight refueling could extend the range beyond the normal maximum of 7,750 miles. Range with 10,000 pounds of bombs was 4,900 miles; total bomb capacity was 28,000 pounds. Top speed was 380 mph, and cruising speed was 277 mph. The service ceiling of 40,000 feet was reached at a climb rate of 2,165 feet per minute.

The B-50C was reclassified as the B-54, details of which are included under that listing.

The last of the B-50 Superfortress type was the TB-50H trainer of which 24 were made. Thus ended a series of bombers that had served their country in two wars.

MARTIN
XB-51

Fig. 198. The first XB-51 during an engine runup.

The Martin Model 234 was originally conceived to fit the role of a high speed ground attack plane, and as such was given the designation XA-45. When the attack classification was abandoned by the Air Force, the design was relabeled XB-51 although the role of ground support remained the same.

Two prototypes were authorized and were given serial numbers 46-685 and -686 -- the first to fly on October 28, 1949. Its diminutive wings had a span of only 53 feet 1 inch and were swept 35 degrees, with an area of 548 square feet. The pilot could vary the angle of incidence of the wing and thus overcome the nose high take-off and landing attitudes common to swept wing aircraft. The most unorthodox feature of the aircraft, however, was the use of three jet engines. Two General Electric J47-GE-13 engines of 5,200 pounds of thrust were podded on pylons attached to the forward fuselage. The third engine was mounted in the tail,

drawing its air from a broad dorsal scoop that faired into the rudder. These engines gave a top speed of 645 mph and a cruising speed of 532 mph. Rate of climb was 6,980 fpm.

Due to the extremely thin wing with variable angle of attack feature, the new bicycle type landing gear was adopted, as used on the earlier XB-48. Full span flaps were incorporated into the wing with spoilers on top of the wings for achieving the necessary roll.

Two men were carried in the fuselage -- the pilot under a bubble canopy, and the radio operator sat behind him under a flush window.

Overall length of the tri-motored attack bomber was 85 feet 1 inch, and the "Tee" tail was 17 feet 4 inches high. Empty weight was 29,584 pounds; gross weight, 55,932 pounds; fuel capacity, 3,535 gallons; service ceiling, 40,500 feet; maximum range, 1,600 miles.

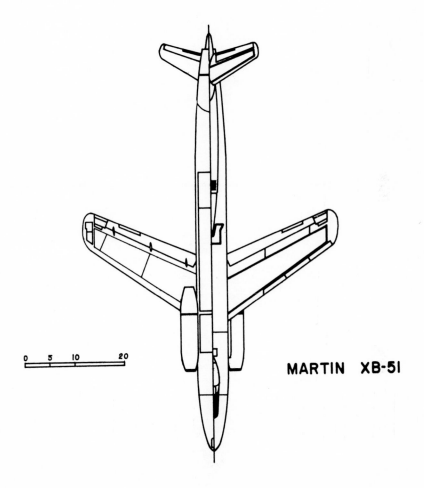

MARTIN XB-5I

0 5 10   20

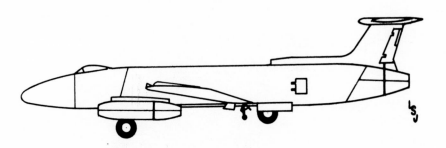

Fig. 199. Martin XB-51.

Fig. 200. Martin's XB-51 was originally planned as a low level attack bomber, designated XA-45.

BOEING
B-52A AND B-52H STRATOFORTRESS

Fig. 201. Boeing YB-52, first Stratofortress to fly.

The strong arm of American strategic airpower is manifested in the powerful Boeing B-52 series of aircraft. These planes were built as pure jet replacements for the huge B-36's which were fast becoming obsolete in the face of new defensive techniques.

Like the smaller B-47 design, the first suggestions for the new intercontinental bomber had straight wings. However, power was to be supplied by six Wright T-35 prop-jet engines. The first configuration to bear the XB-52 title appeared on the drawing boards in July, 1948, and had the wings swept back by a conservative 20 degrees, but still retained the turboprops. On October 27, 1948, the final Stratofortress design was approved with a 35 degree sweep to the wings and eight of the new Pratt & Whitney J57-P-3 jets capable of 9,000 pounds of thrust suspended below them.

On November 29, 1951, the XB-52, concealed beneath tarpaulins, was rolled

from its birthplace. First of the type to fly, though, was the YB-52 (49-231)* on April 15, 1952; the XB-52 following on October 2, 1952. Installation of additional equipment in the first plane necessitated the reversed procedure. The two prototype ships had an approximate empty weight of 155,000 pounds and maximum of 390,000 pounds. Fuel tanks held 38,270 gallons of JP-4, giving a range of 7,000 miles with an offensive load of 10,000 pounds. Top speed exceeded 600 mph, and service ceiling was greater than 50,000 feet. Rate of climb was 2,400 feet per minute.

The production model B-52A was ordered even before completion of the prototypes, and the first of these flew on August 5, 1954. The bubble type canopy used on the X & Y models was replaced by a more conventional cockpit, adding 3 feet to the fuselage length. Newer J57-P-3's with 9,700 pounds of thrust were used. Performance and weights are

*In January of 1958, the YB-52 was presented to the Air Force Museum, Wright-Patterson Air Force Base, Dayton, Ohio.

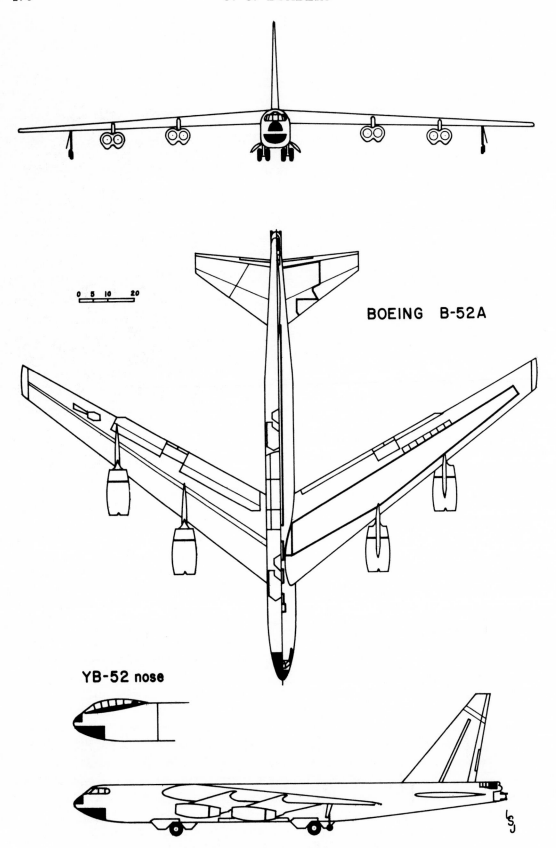

BOEING   B-52A

0 5 10   20

YB-52 nose

Fig. 202. Boeing B-52A Stratofortress.

Fig. 203. First of the three B-52A's, with the "airliner" type cockpit.

Fig. 204. A six engine B-52 was flown on October 11, 1957. Two 15,000 lb thrust Pratt & Whitney J75's replaced the four J57's in the outboard nacelles. The afterburning J75's were mounted for testing purposes on the XB-52. Note the B-52B type wingtip fuel tanks.

classified, but it can be said that the top speed exceeds 650 mph and maximum weight is 350,000 pounds. Service ceiling tops 50,000 feet. Only three B-52A's were built, and two of these are based at Edwards Air Force Base in California as the NB-52A platforms used to launch the X-15's in their epoch making flights into space.

The bulk of America's strategic bomber force is composed of RB-52B's, B-52C's, and later models, quantities of which cannot be disclosed.

The B-52G carries additional offense in the form of two North American GAM-77 Hound Dog jet powered missiles. Defensive armament of this Stratofort consists of four .50 cal. machine guns in the tail directed and fired by closed circuit television. The "G" model was the first B-52 with the rudder shortened by 8 feet. This variation also introduced the "wet" wing, in which the wing itself forms the fuel cell, giving a range of more than 10,000 miles. This can be increased by more than 25 per cent with aerial refueling. The B-52G is powered by eight Pratt & Whitney J57-P-43-W engines with a thrust of 13,750 pounds each with which altitudes of over 60,000 feet can be reached.

At the time of this writing, the newest development of the B-52 series is now beginning production. This is the B-52H, powered by eight Pratt & Whitney TF-33-P-1 turbofan engines of 17,000 pounds thrust. These engines offer a twelve per cent reduction in fuel consumption over the B-52G engines.

Defense from rear attack is provided by an ASG-21 Gatling type rotary cannon. Primary offensive load will consist of four Douglas GAM-87A Skybolt missiles which are carried externally under the wing. These weapons have a range of approximately 1,000 miles and follow a ballistic trajectory to their targets. The Skybolt weighs almost 11,000 pounds.

Like other Boeing types, the B-52 design is adaptable to new developments which provide a modern aircraft at a minimum of expense.

The dimensions of the YB-52 are as follows: span, 185 feet; length, 153 feet; height, 48 feet 4 inches; wing area, 4,000 square feet.

Dimensions of the B-52H are span, 185 feet; length, 157 feet; height, 40 feet 8 inches. All other specifications are classified.

Fig. 205. An NB-52A carrying the X-15 rocket research craft.

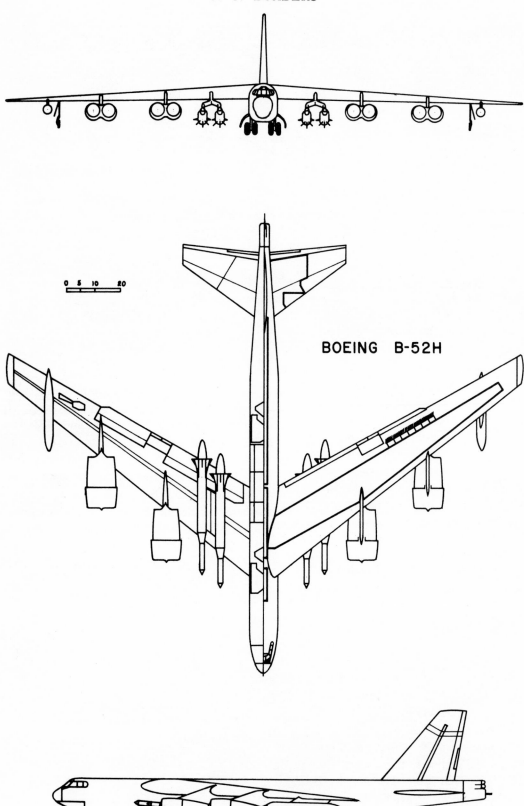

Fig. 206. Boeing B-52H Stratofortress.

Fig. 207. The first B-52H at rollout. Plane carries four Douglas GAM-87A Skybolt ALBM's.

Fig. 208. Note size of intakes on turbofan engines used in the B-52H.

CONVAIR
XB-53

Fig. 209. Clean lines of swept forward XB-53 are apparent on this model.

Undoubtedly, the most unusual configuration to be classed as a bomber was the Convair XB-53. This curious design was a result of reports on German tests with forward swept wings during World War II.

In 1945, Convair began design studies for a fast attack bomber using the new wing principle. This was given the Air Force designation XA-44, and development funds were procured from the XB-46 program. The project was renamed XB-53 in 1948. As the design progressed, authorization was given to complete two prototypes (serial numbers 45-59583 and -59584) but the development program was cancelled before the airframes were finished.

The XB-53 wing was swept forward thirty degrees with eight degrees of dihedral, and incorporated a variable incidence tip which deflected twenty degrees upward. Elevators were located inboard on the trailing edge of the wing, and the conventional ailerons were mounted on the deflecting tip section. Flaps filled the space between.

The broad oval fuselage held three 4,000 pound thrust General Electric J35 jets drawing air through two lateral intakes -- one-third of the air being ducted to the engine in the tail. Two retractable turrets were located above and below, aft of the cockpit. A crew of two were to be carried in the attack version with a ''solid'' nose. In the bomber configuration, the XB-53 was to have a four man crew. The bomb bay could hold twelve 1,000 pound bombs, and underwing fittings mounted 40 five inch HVAR rockets. The attack version had a total of 20 .50 cal. guns. The proposed top speed was 583 mph, and service ceiling was figured at 44,000 feet. Maximum range was 2,200 miles; normal was only 875 miles. Internal fuel provisions held 4,335 gallons. Estimated empty weight was 31,760 pounds and loaded was 60,000 pounds.

The XB-53 had a wing span of 80 feet 6½ inches, and an area of 1,370 square feet. Length was 79 feet 6 inches, and height was 23 feet 8 inches.

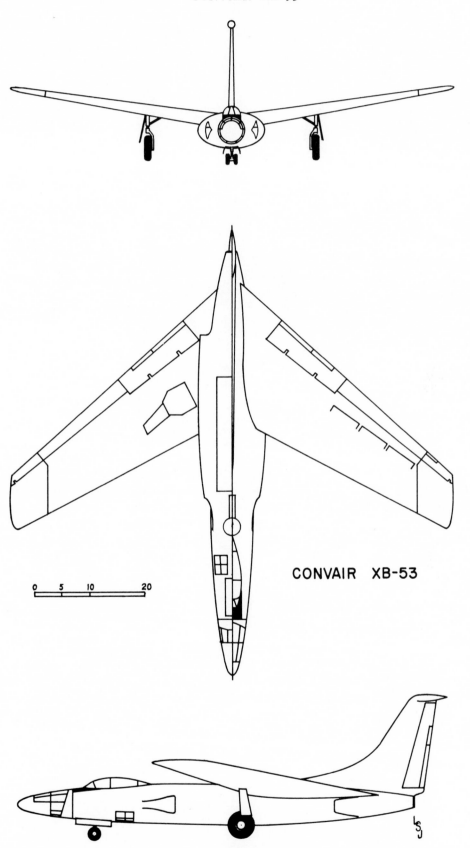

Fig. 210. Convair XB-53.

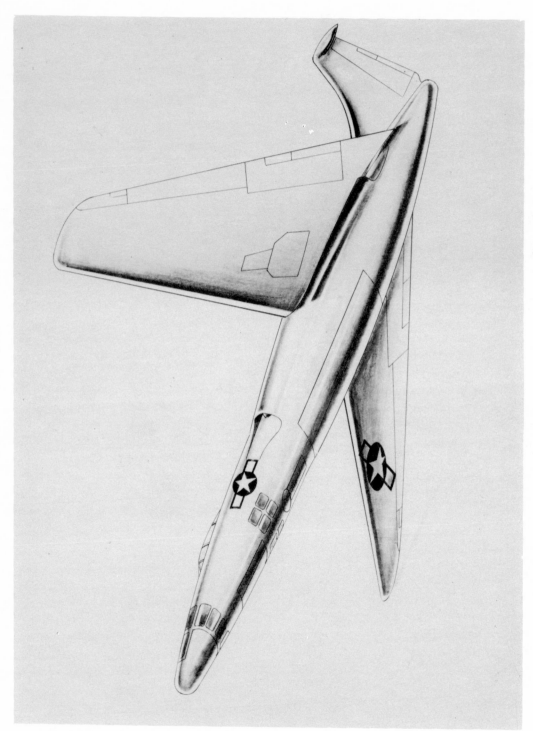

Fig. 211. Artist's impression of Convair XB-53 attack bomber.

BOEING
B-54A

Fig. 212. Note additional outrigger wheels on model of Boeing B-54A.

The story of the B-54 began early in 1947 when Boeing engineers proposed to the Air Force a greatly improved development of the B-50 Superfortress. The new model was to be known as the B-50C and featured the following: wing span increased 20 feet (four feet inboard and six feet at the tips), fuselage lengthened 10 feet 10 inches for a larger bomb capacity, and increasing the engine horsepower to 4,500. This would make a gross weight of 230,000 pounds and extra space for fuel would give a range of 9,300 miles.

The prototype was to be a modified B-50 with unaltered engines. On May 29, 1948, the Air Force ordered seven planes to be designated B-54A and twenty-three as RB-54A for photo reconnaissance. Work began on the prototype at Seattle, but on April 18, 1949, the contract was cancelled before the first plane was completed.

The B-54A was to be powered by the new Pratt & Whitney R-4360-51 VDT Wasp Major engines (for details on this

engine, see YB-36C) giving it a top speed of 433 mph, a cruising speed of 304 mph, and a service ceiling of 40,000 feet. Normal range was to be 4,000 miles. Fuel capacity was 9,320 gallons in the wing with an additional 3,000 gallons in huge external tanks. With auxiliary tanks in the bomb bay, a total of 14,292 gallons could be carried.

The increased weight brought about by the larger engines and airframe modifications necessitated the installation of outrigger wheels in the outboard engine nacelles. The entire aircraft structure was strengthened to withstand the extra weight and greater proportions, but it was estimated that the increased empty weight would not be much more than the rest of the B-50 series.

The wing span of the B-54A was 161 feet 2 inches, length was 111 feet, and height was 32 feet 8 inches. Armament consisted of ten .50's in remote barbettes and four in a manned tail position.

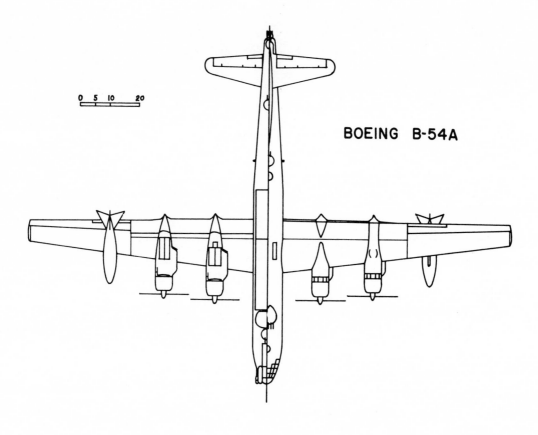

BOEING   B-54A

0 5 10   20

Fig. 213. Boeing B-54A.

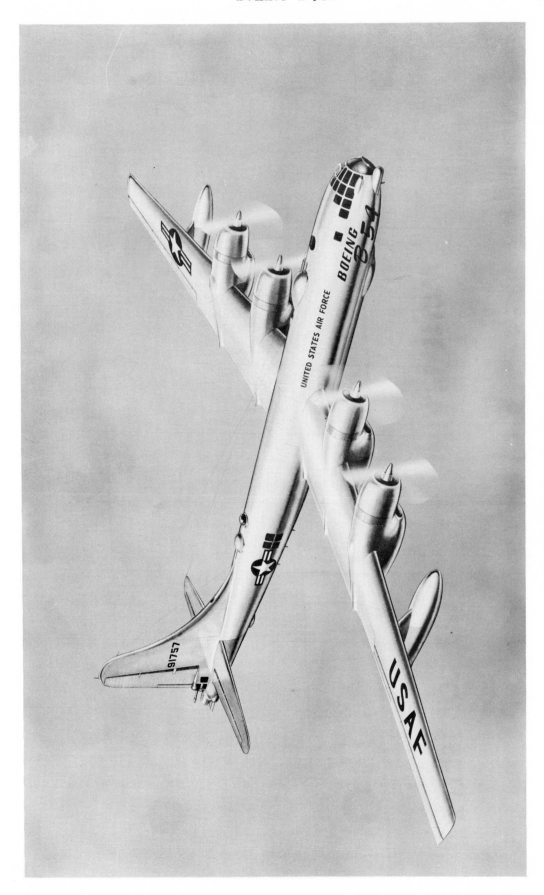

Fig. 214. Drawing shows Boeing B-54A, final development of the Superfortress series.

BOEING
XB-55

Fig. 215. This photo shows a model of the unbuilt XB-55 turboprop bomber planned by Boeing in 1949.

The only fully turbo-prop powered design to bear a U. S. A. F. Bomber designation is Boeing's Model 474, or XB-55. This bomber was proposed to the U. S. A. F. in 1949 but did not progress beyond the blueprint stage. Although somewhat enlarged, the XB-55 design bore a strong resemblance to the all jet B-47 then reaching operational status.

Four Allison T40-A2 turbo-prop engines were mounted on pylons beneath the moderately swept wing and were to deliver 5,643 shaft horsepower each to the six-bladed contraprops. With this power, the top speed was estimated at 490 mph. Cruising speed was to be 452 mph with a service ceiling of 42,100 feet. Range of the XB-55 was to extend to 5,333 miles with a fuel load of 9,500 gallons. The bomb bay could encase a variety of loads such as four 4,000 pound bombs, twelve 1,600 pound or 2,000 pound bombs, twenty-four 1,000 pound types, or forty 500 pound bombs. It was proposed to arm the XB-55 with a total of twelve 20 mm cannons mounted in three turrets. Provisions were made for ten crewmen.

Dimensions of the propjet bomber show a wing span of 135 feet with an area of 1,500 square feet, a length of 118 feet 10.8 inches, and a height of 33 feet 8 inches. Projected empty weight was 78,020 pounds, gross being 153,000 pounds. Maximum alternate gross was 168,000 pounds.

The planned performance of the Boeing XB-55 was overshadowed by that of the large pure jet designs then on the drawing boards or about to enter service, therefore no production was undertaken for the turboprop powered ship.

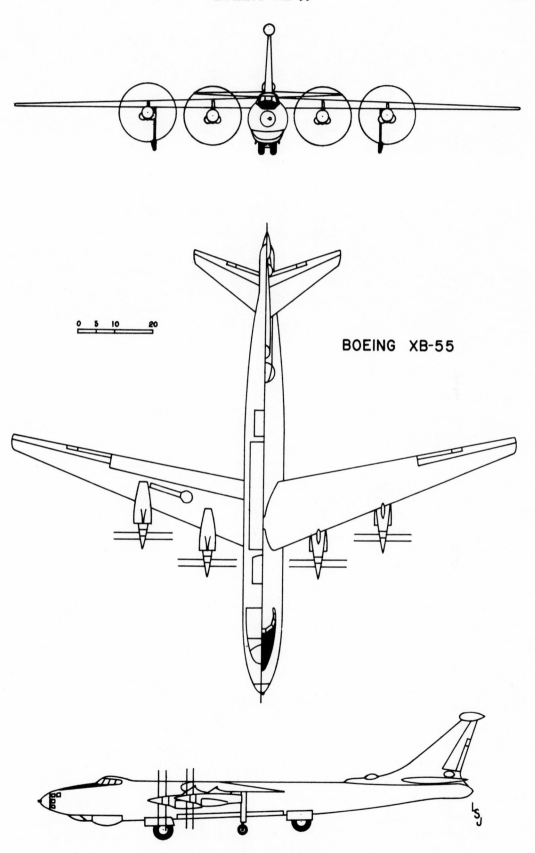

0 5 10   20

BOEING XB-55

Fig. 216. Boeing XB-55.

Fig. 217. Tail barbettes were to mount a total of twelve 20mm cannons fired by remote control.

BOEING
XB-56 STRATOJET

Fig. 218. A model of the Boeing XB-56, four engine version of the Stratojet.

Early in 1950, Boeing proposed their Model 450-19-10, a revised B-47 Stratojet, to be powered by four Allison J35-A-23 engines of 10,090 pounds of thrust each. The four engine design received the designation XB-56 from the Air Force but it was eventually relabeled YB-47C and the earlier designation cancelled.

The most apparent change of the XB-56 configuration is the removal of one engine from the inboard pod. To compensate for the reduced weight and resulting change in the center of gravity, the single J35 was mounted further forward of the wing. The stabilizing outrigger wheels retracted into the pylons. The aileron was located entirely inboard of the outer engine nacelle, the dual type used on the B-47 being eliminated.

The estimated top speed of the XB-56 is classified, but it can be rated at over 600 mph. Range was to be in excess of 3,000 miles with a service ceiling over 40,000 feet. As in the B-47, the XB-56 was to carry a crew of three men. The dimensions were basically the same as B-47B -- span was 116 feet, wing area was 1,428 square feet, length was 106 feet 10.2 inches, and height was 27 feet 10.6 inches. More than ten tons of bombs could be carried.

Further proposals for the XB-56, or YB-47C, suggested use of four Allison J71's in place of the J35's, but none of the modifications materialized and the four engine Stratojet remained a blueprint bomber.

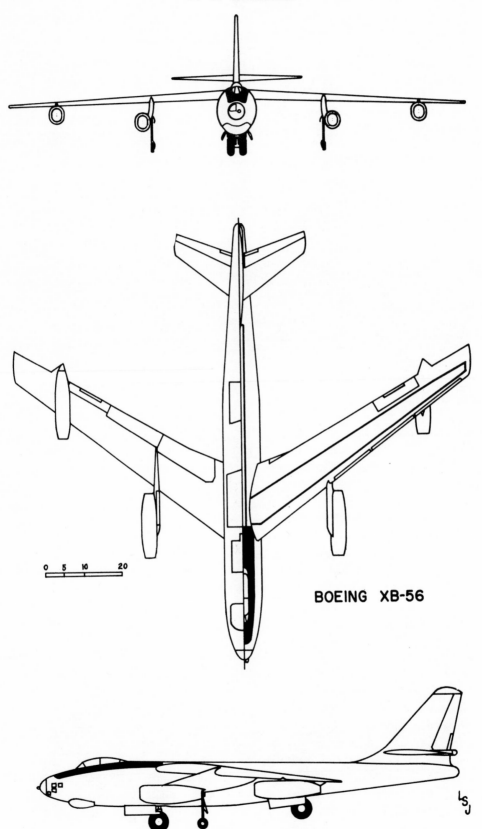

BOEING XB-56

0 5 10   20

Fig. 219. Boeing XB-56 Stratojet.

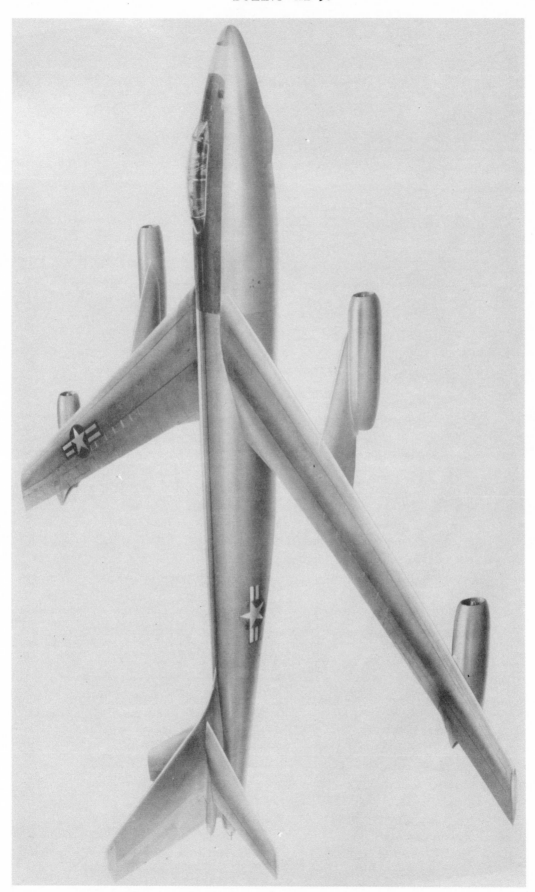

Fig. 220. This is an artist's impression of the XB-56, or YB-47C medium bomber.

MARTIN
B-57B INTRUDER

Fig. 221. Martin's B-57B Intruder shows its capability of carrying a heavy offensive load.

The Martin Model 272 is one of the few American combat aircraft to have its origin in a foreign country. While seeking a bomber to fit the still unfilled position of assault and ground attack plane, the U. S. Air Force was attracted to the performance of the British designed English Electric Canberra. This twin jet design reflected a viewpoint quite opposite to that of American engineers -- short stubby wings with a broad chord, and the engines mounted through the wings. The performance, though, was what the Air Force had been seeking, and in March of 1951, the Martin Company was given a production order for an American development of the Canberra design. The first one flew on July 20, 1953.

Given the name Intruder, the B-57A bears only an external similarity to its British counterpart due to an extensive structural redesign to conform to Air Force specifications. The B-57B has a conventional bubble canopy instead of the Canberra "bowl" type. The plane is operated by two crewmen. Power to achieve a top speed of 580 mph (Mach 0.83) is supplied by two Wright J65-W-5 engines of 7,200 pounds of thrust. Rate of climb is 3,500 feet per minute, and service ceiling is 48,000 feet. Range is normally 2,300 miles, but can be extended to 2,650 miles. Empty weight is 30,000 pounds and it grosses at 49,500 pounds.

The B-57A mounts no guns, but the B-57B can carry four 20 mm cannon or eight .50 cal. machine guns supplimented by air to ground rockets and bombs in underwing loads. Additional bombs are carried within the fuselage on the rotary bomb door.

The B-57C is a dual-control modification for training, and the B-57E can tow aerial targets or serve as an operational bomber.

Dimensions of the B-57B are: span, 64 feet; length, 65 feet 6 inches; height, 15 feet 7 inches; wing area, 960 square feet.

The number of B-57 type bombers to be delivered before the conclusion of production amounts to 403 units.

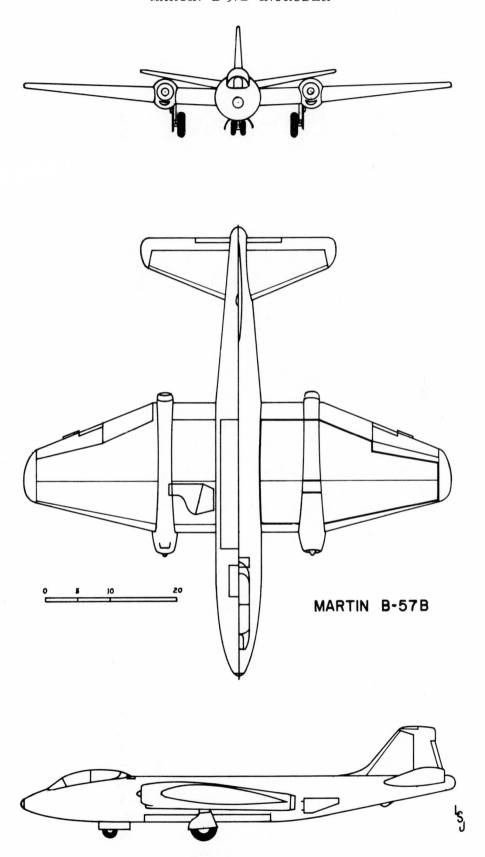

MARTIN B-57B

Fig. 222. Martin B-57B Intruder.

MARTIN
RB-57D

Fig. 223. The RB-57D is a high altitude reconnaissance ship carrying one man. In the background is a B-57A with the conventional wing.

The RB-57D is an extremely high altitude, long range development of the Intruder line. Its uses have ranged from high altitude engine test bed to photo reconnaissance missions of long duration.

While the fuselage remains pretty much the same as other models of the B-57 series, the nose carries either an extensively outfitted camera bay or electronic equipment. As a photo plane, the RB-57D can carry trimetrogen, vertical, forward, and oblique camera mountings. A service ceiling of over 60,000 feet is the result of the disproportionately long wing which spans 109 feet 6 inches and the use of two 9,700 pound thrust Pratt & Whitney J57-P-5 engines. The RB-57D has an approximate top speed of 675 mph at sea level and 590 mph at altitude.

At least three different versions of the "D" are known to exist; each of them being single seat craft. However, no further information can be published.

Specific speed, range, and altitude figures for the RB-57D's are classified, but is is quite clear they exceed those of the "standard" models. The 109 foot wing span varied with the installation of wingtip mounted radar packages. Overall length is 65 feet 6 inches, and height is 15 feet 7 inches.

An interesting feature of the long wing is the location of the ailerons at the half span. This positioning reduces any tendencies to cause wing twisting and control reversal at the high speeds imposed on such a flexible wing.

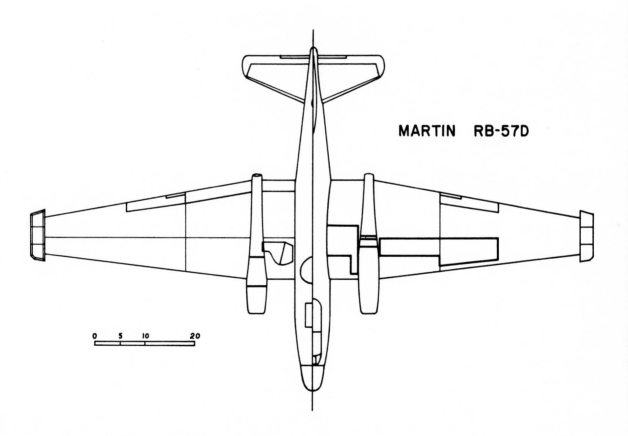

MARTIN   RB-57D

0   5   10   20

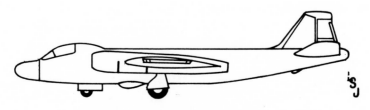

Fig. 224. Martin RB-57D Intruder.

Fig. 225. Engine nacelles on the RB-57D are larger to house J57 engines.

CONVAIR
B-58A HUSTLER

Fig. 226. Convair XB-58 Hustler, first supersonic bomber.

No bomber has made such a definite break with the past as Convair's B-58. Entirely new in concept, the Hustler introduces the dramatic new era of supersonic flight to strategic bombing. An airplane capable of delivering a bomb load at twice the speed of sound had to be different.

The original proposal for the delta winged ship was made in 1949 in a design competition requiring an airplane able to deliver a nuclear package at supersonic speed. Following a development program, the original design was greatly modified to utilize the new area rule principle and a conical-cambered wing. These design formulas dictated a fuselage so slim that it would be impractical to use a conventional bomb bay arrangement. Instead, a weapons pod was attached to carry offensive loads. On October 13, 1954, Convair received a contract for the construction of thirteen prototypes.

But more than the shape of the Hustler is radical. Most of the structure is covered by panels of honeycomed skin. This con-

sists of two sheets of aluminum bonded to a honeycomb of fibreglass or aluminum. The minute air spaces allow the skin to withstand the high temperatures caused by supersonic air friction.

The first B-58 (55-660) flew on November 11, 1956, with four General Electric J79-GE-1 engines. These powerplants have a normal rating of 10,500 pounds of thrust, but are boosted to 16,000 pounds with afterburning. Like its contemporaties, the Hustler carries its engines in underslung pods. Later models use the J-79-GE-5B.

The three crewmen ride in a missile-like fuselage along with one of the most advanced navigation and bomb aiming systems ever assembled -- the Sperry AN/ASQ-42V. This system provides the exact aircraft location, speed, altitude, and distance to the target; and a Bendix autopilot provides complete automatic control. A variety of weapons can be carried beneath the fuselage in the detachable pod.

Performance specifications of the B-58

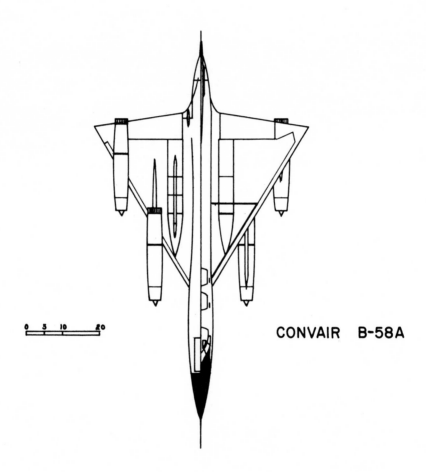

CONVAIR   B-58A

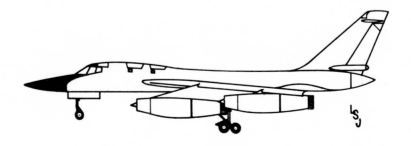

Fig. 227. Convair B-58A Hustler.

Fig. 228. The conical camber on the Hustler wing can be seen in this view. One of the many different weapons pods is shown.

Fig. 229. The Hustler's high landing speed requires the use of a parabrake. Note the eighteen wheel landing gear.

are classified, but at this writing, the Hustler has made seven major speed records including a closed course run of 1,302 mph, or almost eleven times faster than the top speed of the Keystone XB-1! The service ceiling is in the vicinity of 60,000 feet, and range can be extended by aerial refueling. Estimated gross weight of the B-58 is 160,000 pounds.

A single General Electric T-171E Vulcan 20 mm rotary cannon offers an effective rear guard. The plane's tremendous speed serves as additional defense.

The conical camber employed in the design of the wing aids in the remarkable performance of this airplane. The name comes from the shape of the leading edge, which is rolled downward as if over a cone, with the apex at the root and the base at the wing tip. The extremely thin wing does not provide sufficient space for conventional landing gear. To reduce the overall bulk, the main supports consist of eight wheels on each spidery strut. The bogies retract snuggly into Vee shaped fairings raised out of the wing surfaces.

For all its capabilities, the B-58 is not a large aircraft; its delta wing spreading 56 feet 10 inches, with an area of 1,542 square feet. Length is 96 feet 9 inches; height, 31 feet 5 inches.

BOEING
XB-59

Fig. 230. An unusual feature for an American jet aircraft was the buried engines in the wing root as shown on this model of the XB-59.

A parallel proposal for a supersonic bomber was offered by Boeing to the Air Force at the same time Convair was showing the XB-58 proposal. This design bore the Boeing model number 701 and was assigned the Air Force weapons system designation MX-1965, or XB-59.

The XB-59 was to incorporate a short span, broad chord wing, almost delta in appearance. Four buried General Electric J73-X24A engines of approximately 9,300 pounds of thrust were to have afterburners boosting thrust to 14,000 pounds each. With this power, it was estimated that the XB-59 would have Mach 2 capabilities. Top speed was to be 1,200 mph. Typical of contemporary Boeing bomber design was the bicycle landing gear and wingtip mounted outriggers. The extremely clean airframe had a proposed empty weight of 63,200 pounds with a 148,300 pound gross. This would include up to 14,200 pounds of bombs, 10,533 gallons of fuel, and three crew members. The XB-49 had a projected range of 2,380 nautical miles and a service ceiling of 51,000 feet. Armament consisted of a single 30 mm tail-mounted gun.

The stubby swept wing was shoulder mounted and spanned 81 feet 4 inches. Wing area was 1,650 square feet. A length of 123 feet 4 inches with the small rudder reaching a height of 25 feet 4 inches gave the XB-59 design a lean appearance in keeping with its planned performance.

The XB-59 project was surpassed by more advanced aircraft and missile programs and the Boeing Model 701 became simply a design study.

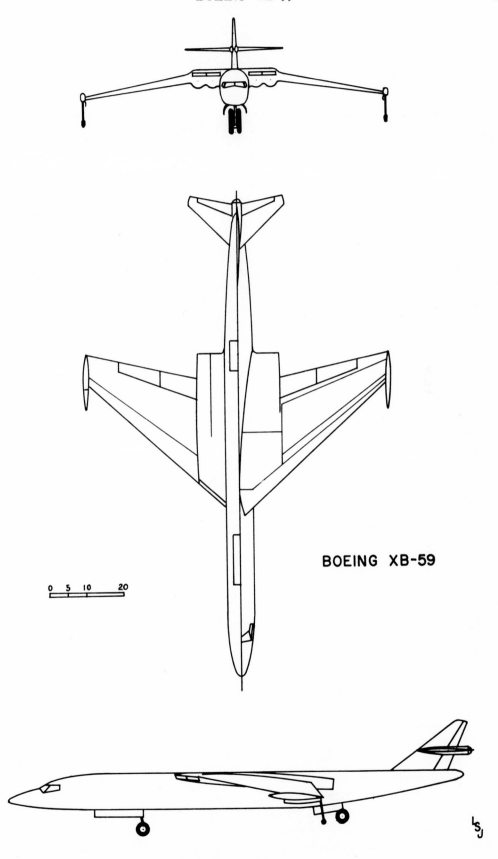

BOEING XB-59

0 5 10   20

Fig. 231. Boeing XB-59.

CONVAIR
YB-60

Fig. 232. Convair's YB-60 was the largest pure jet airplane to fly.

While the Air Force was seeking a jet replacement for the slower B-36 during the early 1950's, the engineers at Convair proposed an all jet version of the big ship. This was to be known as the B-36G and make use of much of the tooling and components of the prop driven model. On March 15, 1951, the Air Force authorized construction of two prototypes, designating them YB-60's.

When the first plane was ready for its initial flight on April 18, 1952, its descendancy from the B-36 was quite apparent. The same tubular fuselage, however, was tapered to a needle pointed instrument boom in the nose, and was topped by a large swept vertical stabilizer on the tail. The B-36 wing center section with the landing gear assembly was used. In fact, the airplane serial number 49-2676 had been originally assigned to a B-36D. The wing sweepback reduced the overall span to 206 feet. The eight J57-P-3 engines had a thrust rating

of 9,000 pounds and were paired in underwing pods, typical of American engineering philosophy concerning engine mounting. This arrangement used the engine pods as mass counterbalances on the flexible wing. (In contrast, British engineers encase the engines entirely within the wing structure.)

Flight testing showed that the thicker wing, greater bulk, and heavier airframe did not give comparable performance to the new B-52 being tried at the same time. The top speed did not exceed 520 mph; service ceiling was approximately 45,000 feet. Range was 8,000 miles, and the loaded weight came to about 300,000 pounds. Empty weight is estimated at 150,000 pounds. The crew was made up of ten men.

The YB-60 had a wing span of 206 feet, length of 171 feet, and stood 50 feet high, making it the largest all jet aircraft in the world.

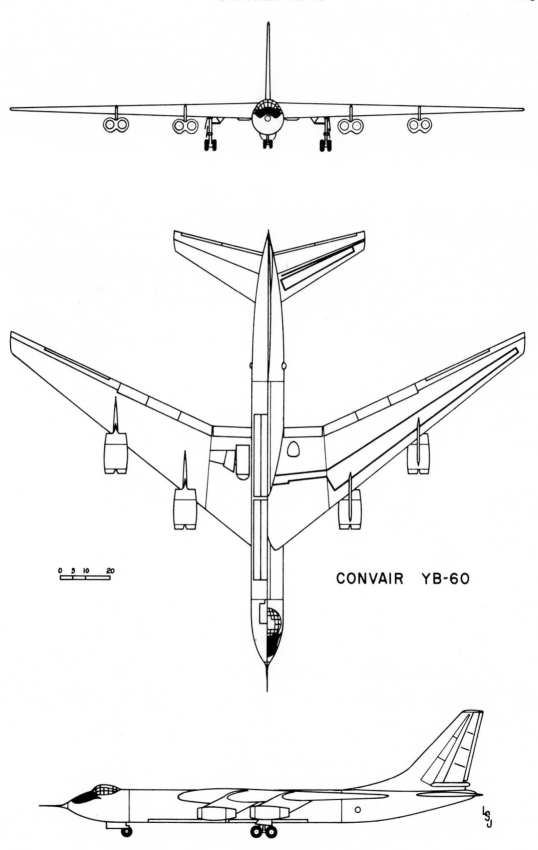

CONVAIR YB-60

0 5 10   20

Fig. 233. Convair YB-60.

Fig. 234. YB-36 wing and fuselage center sections were adapted from a B-36D. Figures show huge size of plane.

Fig. 235. Performance of the YB-60 fell short of the Air Force requirements. The needle nose housed test instruments.

MARTIN
TM-61C MATADOR

Fig. 236. An operational Matador on its mobile launching platform.

The pilotless bomber represents a whole new outlook in the field of strategic aircraft, for here is an airplane designed from the beginning to effect its own destruction. Each flight is a oneway trip! The Martin TM-61 Matador is the first weapon of this concept since the dreaded German V-1 Buzz Bomb of World War II.

Engineering work began in 1946 when the Air Force expressed a need for unmanned types to suppliment conventional bombers. In some circumstances, the costs and risks of manned operation are excessively high, and a self-guided aircraft would provide an effective means of delivering an offensive load at a reasonable cost. Since there would be no landing stress imposed, the structure could be light yet permit heavy loading.

The first example of this weapon was known as the XB-61 and was launched on January 20, 1949. The production articles that followed became the first tactical missiles to be incorporated in the defense arsenal of the United States.

The Matador is fairly orthodox in shape, with a single Allison J33-A-37 engine mounted in the tail to give a thrust of 5,200 pounds. Air for the engine enters an intake located in the fuselage belly. Zero length take-off power is boosted by use of a single solid fuel rocket, which is jettisoned following the launch. The TM-61's transporter serves as its launching platform.

The Matador's tactical range is 600 miles at a speed of 650 mph. However, during the final death dive into the target, supersonic speed is reached. Operational altitude is above 40,000 feet.

The TM-61 has a launch weight of 13,800 pounds, wing span of 28 feet 8 inches, length of 39 feet 6 inches, and a height of 10 feet.

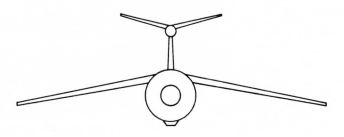

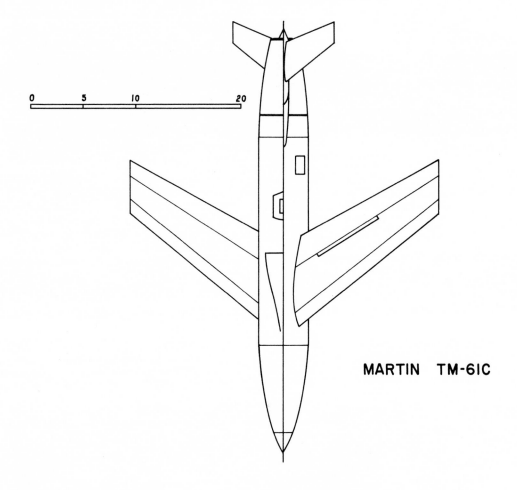

MARTIN   TM-6IC

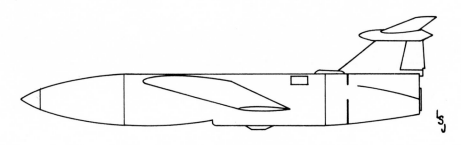

Fig. 237. Martin TM-61C Matador.

Fig. 238. The TM-61 uses a single auxiliary rocket for additional take-off boost.

NORTHROP
SM-62A SNARK

Fig. 239. Due to the absence of a horizontal stabilizer, Northrop's Snark flies in a nose high attitude.

The SM-62 was the second missile type bomber to enter service with the U.S.A.F. However, its performance does not duplicate, but rather augments, that of the TM-61. The Northrop "bird" has true intercontinental range, and a typical mission could be compared to that of a B-47 or B-52, although its cost is but a fraction of the manned types.

The Snark is a semi-tailless air breathing aircraft powered by a Pratt & Whitney J57 engine of 11,000 pounds of thrust giving it a cruise speed of 615 mph at an operational ceiling above 60,000 feet. The missile flies in a nose high attitude due to the absence of a horizontal stabilizer, the function of this unit being taken over by elevons (carryovers from the Flying Wing series of aircraft produced by this company). A range of 5,500 miles is covered by the use of two auxiliary fuel tanks mounted beneath the wings.

Launching of the SM-62 (Strategic Missile) is similar to the manner used for the Matador. The power of the jet engine is aided by a pair of 130,000 pound thrust rocket boosters, which release after take-off. The pilotless bomber climbs to altitude on its jet engine and is guided on a predetermined course to the target area. Its inertial guidance system is periodically checked by a star-tracking device to assure that this course remains accurate. When the destination is reached, the Snark begins a supersonic dive, during which the nose warhead is separated from the airframe. The remainder of the missile, no longer stable, buffets violently until it falls into pieces, which confuse defensive radar systems in the target area.

Firing weight of this weapon is 59,936 pounds. Wing span is 42 feet, length 67 feet, height 15 feet.

Early test vehicles of this machine were fitted with retractable skids for recovery following evaluation flights. The vehicle could then be reflown to test new new components and systems.

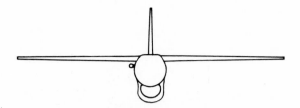

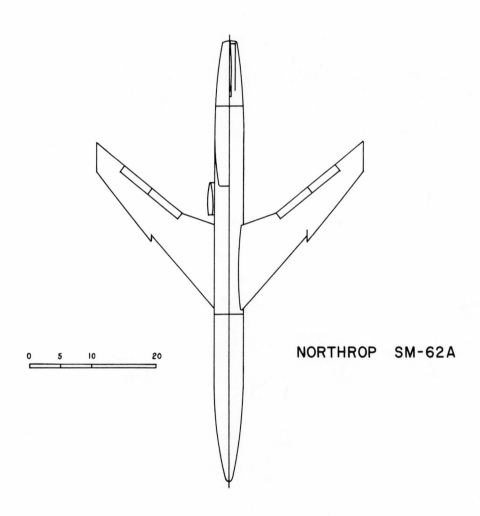

NORTHROP   SM-62A

0   5   10   20

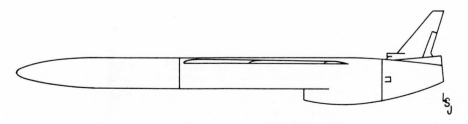

Fig. 240. Northrop SM-62A Snark.

Fig. 241. For additional range, the SM-62 can be fitted with auxiliary underwing fuel tanks.

Fig. 242. Supersonic shock waves are emitted from the twin booster rockets during launching.

BELL
GAM-63 RASCAL

Fig. 243. A Boeing YDB-47E Stratojet was used to transport the Rascal on the first part of its journey.

As guided missile development increased, it became apparent that some of the airplanes they would replace could be used as airborne launching platforms, permitting the missile to be dispatched much closer to the target. Thus carried, much of the expensive and bulky inertial guidance systems could be eliminated and a greater payload included.

With this in mind, Bell Aircraft Company developed the GAM-63 (Guided Air Missile) for the Strategic Air Command. The Rascal, as it is called, was to be carried on an attachment on the fuselage of a Boeing YDB-47E Stratojet and air launched seventy-five miles from its target. As soon as the missile was free of the bomber, the latter would return to its base.

Meanwhile, the 18,200 pound missile would accelerate to almost twice the speed of sound. To achieve this speed, a Bell three-chamber liquid rocket was installed. The Rascal could cruise at 1,000 mph at over 50,000 feet before diving into its target. Although the GAM-63 project was cancelled on September 9, 1958, its concept was retained in such air-launched missiles as the GAM-77 Hound Dog and GAM-87 Skybolt used with the B-52G & H.

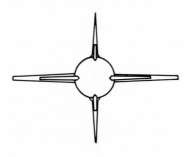

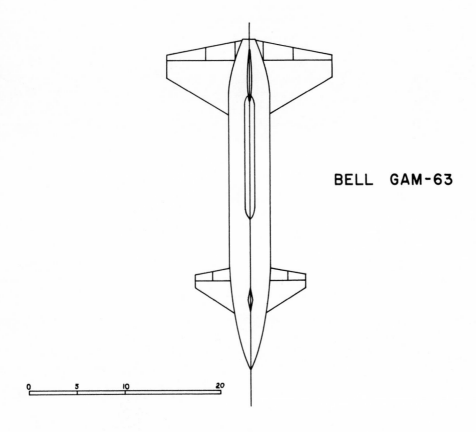

BELL GAM-63

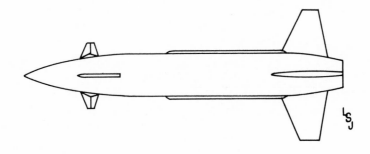

Fig. 244. Bell GAM-63 Rascal.

Fig. 245. The small vertical fins on the nose served as rudders for the GAM-63.

The lower fin of the Rascal folded for ground clearance during handling and mounting of the aircraft. The length of the fuselage was 31 feet 11 inches, span of the rear mounted wing was 16 feet 8 inches, and height with fins extended was 12 feet 6 inches.

For aerodynamic control, ailerons were located on the rear horizontal surfaces -- the elevators being mounted on the nose along with the rudders. The rear vertical surfaces were fixed.

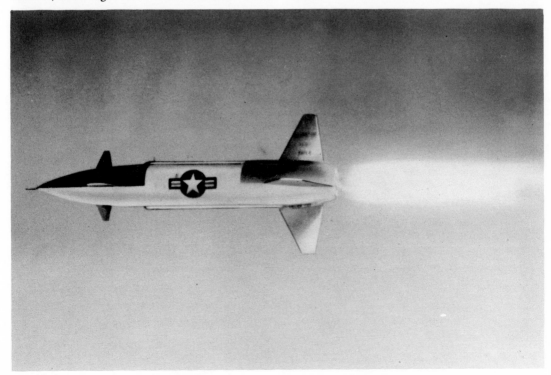

Fig. 246. The Rascal had a cruising speed approaching Mach 2.

NORTH AMERICAN
XSM-64 NAVAHO

Fig. 247. The first of two North American X-10 Navaho test vehicles.

Although the North American Navaho did not reach the production stage, the data gained from its unusual design has had a direct bearing on the development of the B-70 bomber program.

The original flight testing for the Navaho configuration was done on a smaller scale vehicle, designated X-10 by the Air Force. Two such planes were built and were powered by two turbojet engines. A retractable landing gear enabled recovery of the unmanned test vehicles. These scale models of the Navaho had a speed close to Mach 2 and took-off under their own power.

The full scale Navaho, on the other hand, was powered by two North American designed ram jet engines. For launching, the missile was mounted as the second stage to a large liquid rocket booster. Thrust from this booster was sufficient to permit ignition of the ram jet engines. The method of mounting the missile was unique in that it was carried in a piggy-back position on the booster.

Although the XSM-64 had supersonic capabilities and a range comparable to the SM-62, the less radical Snark was awarded the production contract.

Much of the technical data concerning the Navaho has not been disclosed. However, the following information has been released. The booster unit carried 4,193 gallons of lox (liquid oxygen) and 4,330 gallons of alcohol for initial thrust. Booster length was 76 feet 3 inches. Length of the missile itself was 67 feet 10 inches, wing span 28 feet 7 inches, and the height, with landing gear extended, was 17 feet 3 inches. Wing area was 418 square feet. With missile and booster combined, the overall length was 82 feet 5 inches, and height was 21 feet. Fuel capacity of the XSM-64 was 6,360 gallons of JP-5 to provide intercontinental range at supersonic speeds.

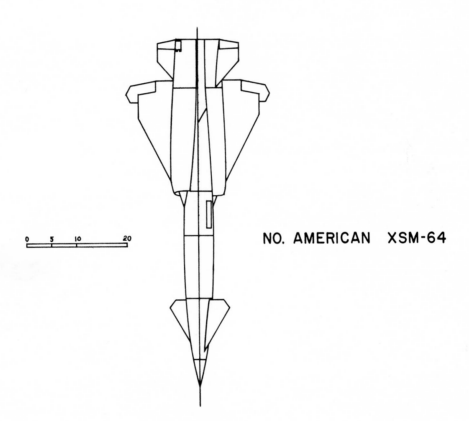

NO. AMERICAN   XSM-64

Fig. 248. North American XSM-64 Navaho.

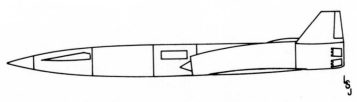

Fig. 249. Piggy-back method of launching the
XSM-64 was unique. Two ramjets sustained
the missile after separation.

Fig. 250. Over 8,500 gallons of fuel were
burned during the launching.

CONVAIR
SM-65D ATLAS

Fig. 251. An early Atlas missile launched on January 10, 1958.

The first intercontinental ballistic missile (ICBM) to reach service in the free world was the SM-65 Atlas. This offensive rocket is the result of a development contract awarded to Convair's Astronautics Division in 1946. The major problem was developing a weapon which could deliver a suitable tactical load to a target some 5,000 miles away. It was not until the development of thermonuclear warheads, that the solution was found. These provided the necessary destructive forces sought, and could be carried in a relatively compact encasement. As a result, the Atlas is about the same length as a contemporary medium bomber.

Construction of this machine is radically different from other defensive weapons. Most notable is the fact that the stainless steel structure is so thin, the tank must be pressurized to support the weight of its own skin -- a veritable steel balloon! Helium is used to obtain pressure up to 10 pounds per square foot.

The SM-65D stands 85 feet 6 inches high including the warhead nose and weighs 260,000 pounds. Power is obtained from three Rocketdyne liquid rocket

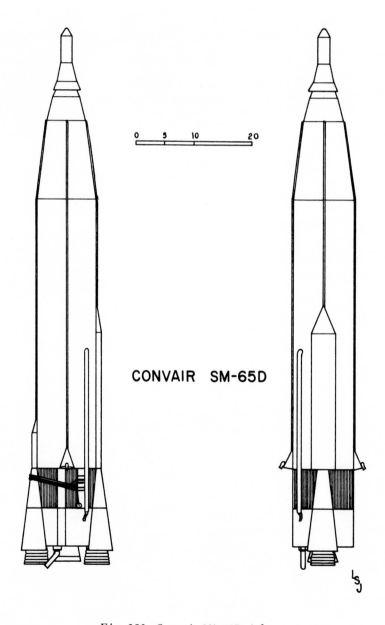

CONVAIR SM-65D

Fig. 252. Convair SM-65D Atlas.

Fig. 253. A Convair SM-65D Atlas intercontinental ballistic missile. Two small rockets on the sides are used for stability.

Fig. 254. First launching of the Atlas-Agena satellite vehicle in the Midas project, May 24, 1960.

engines, two of which drop off with the first stage. The sustainer engine is an LR89-NA-3, the two boosters being LR 105-NA's, giving a total of 360,000 pounds of thrust at lift off. Following the launching, the two boosters and their metal skirt drop away. Two small vernier rockets correct the second stage attitude, while the course is set by the guidance systems located in streamlined fairings on the tank sides.

During its flight, the missile climbs to an altitude of almost 900 miles and arches over to cover a range that has been measured at 6,325 miles, but may exceed 7,900 miles. As the flight nears the end, retro rockets are used to slow the shell from a speed of 16,000 mph and separate the nose cone. Following separation, the cone carrying the warhead continues at this velocity until it strikes the target area.

Not only is the Atlas an effective weapon, it also serves as a satellite launching vehicle for space exploration. On December 18, 1958, an Atlas itself was placed in an orbit lasting 34 days (Project Score).

DOUGLAS
RB-66C DESTROYER

Fig. 255. An RB-66C, one of over 200 Destroyers built for the Air Force.

Following the highly successful tests of the Douglas A3D-1 Skywarrior for the U. S. Navy, the Air Force expressed an interest in a land based version as a fast photo-reconnaissance and attack type. On June 28, 1954, the Air Force's RB-66A (52-2828) was ready for flight testing, and although it resembled the A3D-1, it was an entirely new airplane.

Most noticeable, was an enlarged wing center section and redesigned cockpit canopy. Two slim engine pods each encased an Allison J71-A-11 of 10,200 pounds thrust. Only five RB-66A's were built for evaluation -- the original airframe now serving as a test bed for General Electric engines. The B-66B and RB-66C were both three-place models, and the "D" carried five crewmen. The RB-66C has provisions for aerial refueling via the probe and drogue method. Auxiliary fuel tanks can be fitted beneath the wing-tips to give a maximum range of 1,750 miles.

Fifty-five of the B-66's were delivered as WB-66D's for weather reconnaissance work, including analysis of weather conditions over the combat zone and atmospheric studies for the Air Weather Service.

The Destroyer utilizes a radar bomb aiming system, and mounts two 20 mm cannon in the radar directed General Electric tail stinger. The plane can reach a top speed of 620 mph and has a service ceiling of 43,000 feet. Empty weight is 42,086 pounds, and gross weight comes to 78,000 pounds. Main fuel tanks hold 4,650 gallons. The wing is swept 35 degrees, spans 72 feet 6 inches, and has an area of 780 square feet. Length is 75 feet 1 inch, and height is 23 feet 7 inches.

The fuselage-mounted tricycle landing gear is reminiscent of that used by the earlier XB-43 and permits the use of an exceptionally thin wing. In June of 1958, the 209th B-66 was delivered to the Air Force completing production of the type.

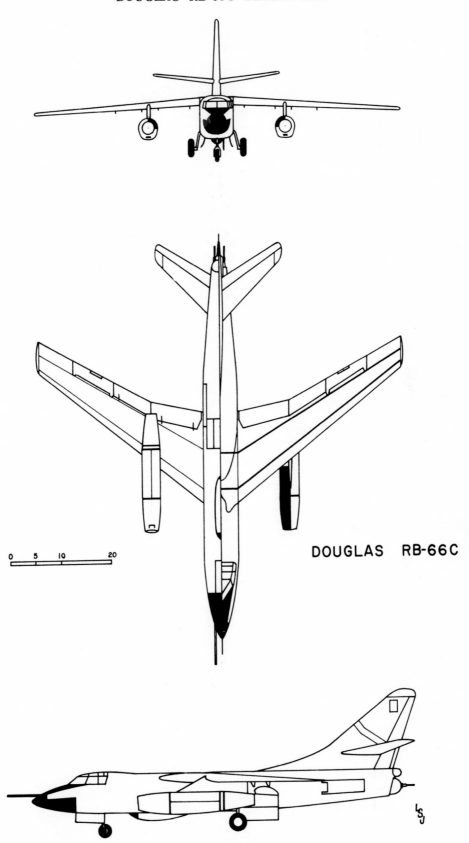

DOUGLAS RB-66C

0   5   10   20

Fig. 256. Douglas RB-66C. Destroyer.

Fig. 257. An RB-66C prepares to couple itself to a KB-50 tanker by the probe and drogue method for aerial refueling.

Fig. 258. A Douglas B-66B Destroyer. The plane is a U.S.A.F. development of the Navy A3D-1 Skywarrior.

RADIOPLANE
GAM-67 CROSSBOW

Fig. 259. Two Radioplane GAM-67's could be carried by the Boeing B-50.

This aircraft seems strangely out of place in a history of bombers, for it is essentially a remotely controlled target drone. However, its adaptability to the role of an electronics counter-measures vehicle merited it the designation GAM-67. Identified by the manufacturer as RP-54D, the Crossbow could be carried by a B-47 or B-50 for air drops, or be rail launched from the ground. Its versitile design permitted a variety of roles ranging from a high altitude target to lower altitude reconnaissance and battlefield surveillance.

Its ability to transmit spurious signals for defensive radar jamming in the target area, or its use as a decoy to lead defending fighters or missiles away from the actual weapon carrier, was particularly useful to the strategic bomber service. The vehicle contained an autopilot and a modified ARW-59 command control receiver system.

On completion of its assigned mission, the GAM-67 would be lowered to earth by a two-stage recovery system using a parabrake and a 54 foot parachute. Landing was made on four plastic impact bags housed in streamlined containers attached to the wings.

One Continental Aviation and Engineering J69-T-17 engine delivered 1,000 pounds of thrust giving the Crossbow a speed of 676 mph at sea level (Mach 0.99). Cruise altitude was 40,000 feet and range was approximately 300 miles. A fuel capacity of 36.2 gallons gave an indurance of 30 minutes.

The tiny missile had an empty weight of 1,650 pounds and grossed 2,800 to 2,900 pounds. An 860 pound payload could be carried. Wing span was 12 feet 6 inches, length 19 feet 1 inch, and height came to 4 feet 6 inches.

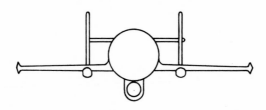

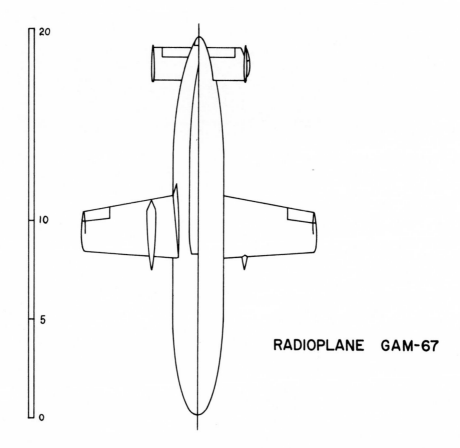

RADIOPLANE GAM-67

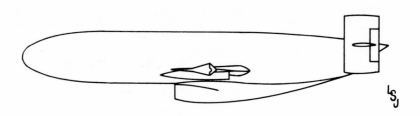

Fig. 260. Radioplane GAM-67 Crossbow.

Fig. 261. Only one of the two rudders was moveable.

Fig. 262. A Crossbow mounted as a decoy on a Boeing Stratojet.

MARTIN
XB-68

Fig. 263. Model of the XB-68 is based on provisional data.

The Martin XB-68 supersonic bomber project was awarded a development contract in September, 1956, as Weapons System 302-A. The design was picked in preference to a competing Douglas proposal.

The XB-68 was to feature a large delta wing mounting two underslung jet pods, similar to the manner displayed by the B-58. A third engine was fuselage mounted, with air being fed through lateral intakes just aft of the two-place cockpit. These powerplants were to be General Electric J79-GE-1 engines giving 10,500 pounds of thrust. Afterburners would increase this to 16,000 pounds. Thus powered, it was estimated the XB-68 would have a speed capability of 1,650 mph (Mach 2.5) and a service ceiling over 50,000 feet.

The project was cancelled early in 1957 before much more than preliminary design studies could be undertaken. The accompanying illustrations are strictly provisional and based upon artists configurations and other limited data that has been released concerning the XB-68. Although the program was cancelled and further development has been abandoned, the project is still classified, and the information contained herein should be considered unofficial.

The B-68 designation was reassigned to the Martin SM-68 Titan missile.

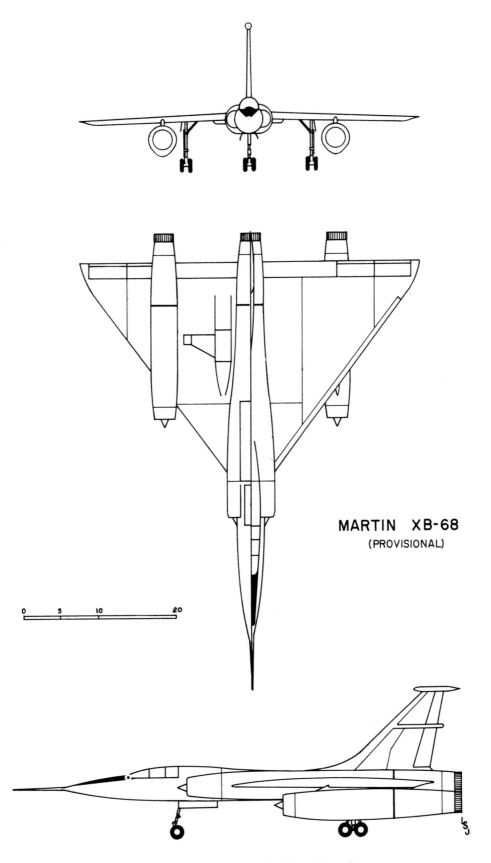

MARTIN XB-68
(PROVISIONAL)

0   5   10   20

Fig. 264. Martin XB-68 (Provisional).

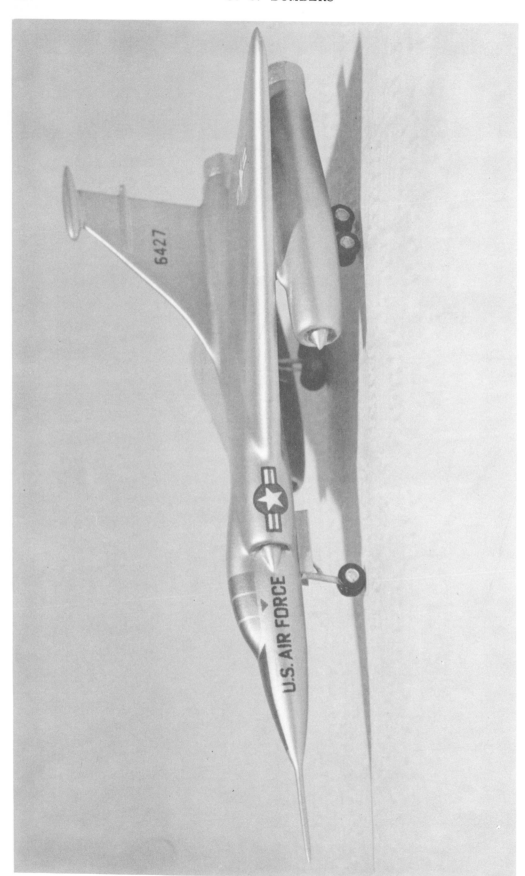

Fig. 265. Martin's XB-68 was a proposed three jet supersonic bomber.

MARTIN
SM-68 TITAN

Fig. 266. The Titan ICBM. Note chips of ice flaking from rocket casing.

The second ballistic missile to reach the production stage is the Martin Titan. Engineering on this ICBM began in 1953, and it was seen as a guarantee against any failure of the SM-65 system. While the development of the Titan parallels its contempary, its method of operation is somewhat different -- a result of experience gained from the Atlas.

The first stage engine of the SM-68 is an Aerojet-General LR87 two chamber unit of 300,000 pounds of thrust. The main chambers are gimballed to produce pitch and yaw control. Following launching, this unit lifts the 220,000 pound missile above the atmosphere where the second stage is separated by four explosive bolts. The weapon coasts for a

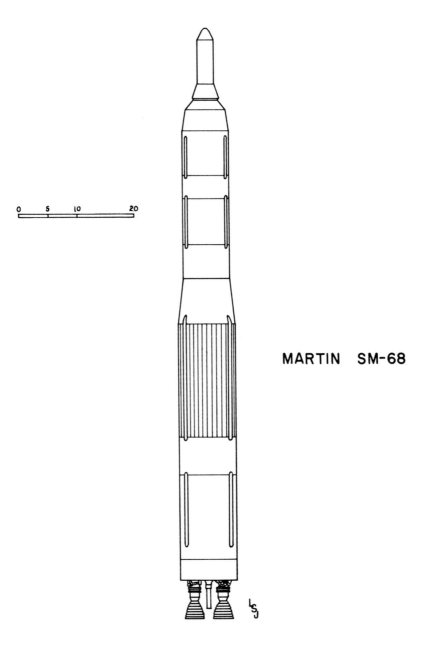

MARTIN   SM-68

Fig. 267. Martin SM-68 Titan.

Fig. 268. The narrow cylinder on the nose of the Titan is the re-entry warhead.

period before the second stage is pulled away from the first by four vernier rockets. An Aerojet-General LR-91 is ignited in space and its 80,000 pound thrust hurls the second stage to a velocity of 17,000 mph. Finally, as the Titan nears its objective, exhaust gasses are diverted forward to divide the nose cone from the missile, and the warhead dives toward its target 15 times faster than the speed of sound.

The name Titan is fitting for the SM-68 as it is the largest ballistic missile known. Height, from rocket chambers to nose cone is 90 to 95 feet, depending on payload installed. Body diameter is 10 feet. In spite of its larger size, the Titan is lighter than its stablemate, the Atlas.

First launching of the SM-68 took place on February 6, 1959, and the warhead has been delivered a distance of 6,333 miles.

LOCKHEED
RB 69A

Fig. 269. The U.S.A.F. RB-69A is a conversion of the Navy P2V-7 Neptune.

Although the existence of the RB-69A has been acknowledged by the U. S. Air Force, details concerning the electronic equipment aboard are classified. However, it is apparent that this version of the Lockheed P2V-7 Neptune carries more equipment than its Navy counterpart by the appearance of the added radome on the MAD boom. In 1954 the Air Force acquired seven P2V-7U patrol bombers from the Navy to be converted for use as radio trainers and reconnaissance aircraft. These planes bear the serial numbers 54-4037 to -4043 and still retain their Navy blue paint scheme.

Externally, the RB-69A is virtually identical to the P2V-7. Two Wright R-3350-32W eighteen cylinder Cyclones of 3,500 horsepower are supplimented by two Westinghouse J34-WE-34 jet engines;

the latter having 3,400 pounds of thrust each -- sufficient to power the RB-69A alone if necessary. Normal top speed is 305 mph, but the jets can increase performance to 356 mph.

The first XP2V-1 flew on May 15, 1945, and the Navy ordered the type into production following the successful testing program. So versatile was the design, that this plane, and later developments of it, have dominated the Navy patrol bomber inventory for more than a decade. In its dual role of Air Force trainer and Navy bomber, the Neptune has a wing span of 103 feet 10 inches. Length is 91 feet 8 inches, and height is 29 feet 4 inches. Wing area is 1,000 square feet. The P2V-7 weighs 47,487 pounds empty and 75,500 pounds gross. The RB-69A weights are comparable. Service ceiling is 31,100 feet and range is 3,850 miles.

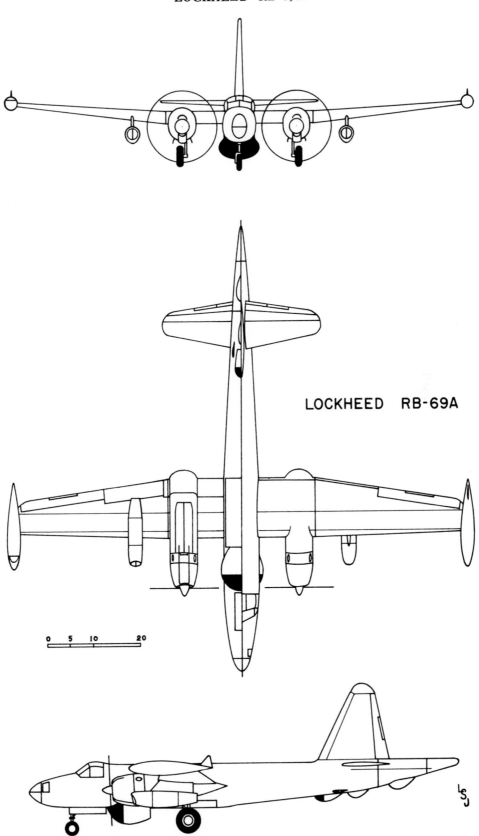

Fig. 270. Lockheed RB-69A Neptune.

Fig. 271. Model of RB-69A conversion of Navy P2V-7U Neptune.

Fig. 272. The Neptune is used as a radio and navagation trainer by the Air Force.

NORTH AMERICAN
XB-70 VALKYRIE

Fig. 273. In supersonic flight the Valkyrie's wingtips were lowered to increase stability.

XB-70 was conceived in 1954 as a subsonic bomber capable of short supersonic dashes. On December 23, 1957, North American won a competition with Boeing for development of the new bomber. By this time supersonic technology had advanced to the point that it became practical to design a heavy bomber able to cruise supersonically for extended periods. Despite the obvious military potential of a Mach 3 bomber, the U.S. government decided to build only two of the big craft, and these were to be used purely for high-speed research.

The first of the two Valkyries was rolled out of its hangar on May 11, 1964 and it presented an awesome appearance unlike any aircraft yet seen. Its design take-off weight was 542,000 lbs. and this included 12,000 lbs. of titanium and 300,000 lbs. of fuel. No less dramatic than its first appearance was the initial flight of the mammoth bomber. On September 21, 1964, its white finish gleaming in the sunlight, the XB-70 was guided down the runway before more than 5,000 spectators and lifted easily

into the air. Then began the first of a series of minor, but troublesome, events which marred the life of this remarkable aircraft. One of the main landing gear bogies failed to rotate prior to retraction and the gear could not be retracted. Plans for a supersonic dash on the first flight had to be cancelled and the XB-70 made an emergency landing at Edwards AFB, its home for the remainder of its operational life.

The second XB-70 joined the flight test program on July 17, 1965 and featured improvements found necessary during testing of the first aircraft.

The XB-70A was powered by six General Electric YJ-93-GE-3 of 30,000 lbs. thrust each, with afterburning. The highest speed attained by the Valkyrie was Mach 3.08 or more than 2,000 mph at 70,000 feet. At this speed it took 13 minutes and an arc of 287 miles in width to complete a 180 degree turn!

A unique characteristic of the Valkyrie's configuration was its ability to ride its own supersonic shock wave, much the same as a

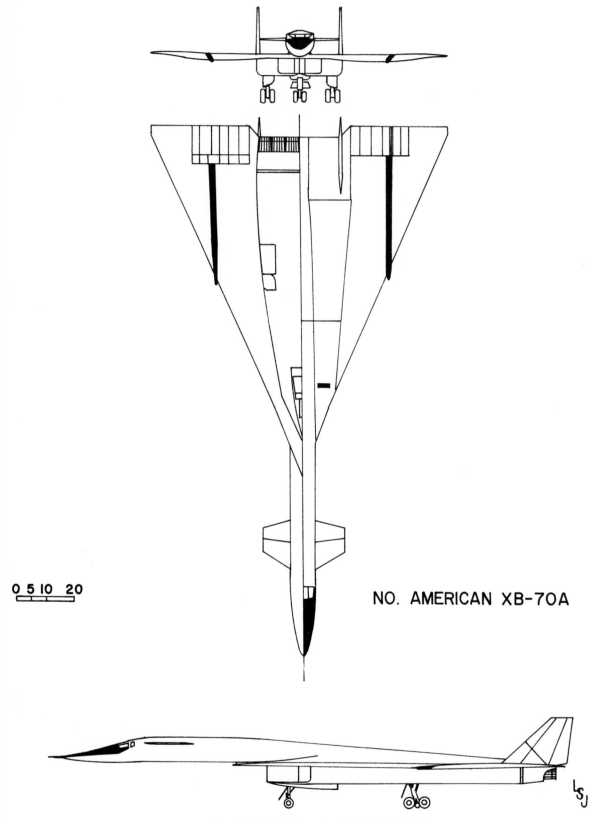

0 5 10 20

NO. AMERICAN XB-7OA

Fig. 274. North American XB-70A Valkyrie.

Fig. 275. XB-70A, wearing NASA trim, lifts off on test flight to provide data for Supersonic Transport program.

Fig. 276. Second XB-70A on landing roll. This ship featured dihedral in outer wing panels.

Fig. 277. Huge delta wing is apparent in this view of the Valkyrie. Note finger type ailerons.

surf board glides on the crest of a wave. Called Compression Lift, this principle markedly reduced drag and was the secret of the XB-70's performance.

A jet engine cannot operate unless incoming air is subsonic. A complex series of baffles was built into the XB-70's intake ducts to set up progressive shock waves to reduce the speed of the incoming air. Less than 100 feet down the intake duct the air was slowed from Mach 3 to Mach 0.5 as it entered the engines.

The Valkyrie's delta wing had an area of 6,300 square feet making it the largest structure of its type yet built. To increase directional stability at high Mach numbers the outer third of each wing was folded downward. This increase of keel area at Mach 3 allowed the size of the rudders to be reduced by more than 50%. Exterior of the plane was tough stainless-steel-honeycomb skin with a specially-prepared heat resistant paint. Recorded skin temperatures during a 21 minute Mach 3 flight reached 620 degrees.

During the peak of the testing program the second Valkyrie was lost in a tragic mid-air collision. The first plane was re-instrumented and for two more years served as a flying laboratory for the American Supersonic Transport program. On February 4, 1969 the remaining XB-70A Valkyrie was delivered to the U.S. Air Force for display at the new Air Force Museum near Dayton, Ohio.

The XB-70A wing spanned 105 feet, overall length was 189 feet, height was 30 feet. The two crew members rode on ejection seats which slid backward into rocket propelled capsules for escape during the entire flight-speed regime.

Fig. 278. Mock-up of B-1A. Small canards on nose are designed to dampen rough ride caused by low-level turbulence.

Missile technology of the late 1950's led many to speculate on the end of the manned bomber, however use of aging B-57's and B-52's during the Vietnam War proved beyond doubt the value of the crewmen being able to assess a given situation and react accordingly.

In June 1970, Rockwell International, successor to North American, was chosen to design America's newest strategic deterent to replace the Boeing B-52. Beginning flight testing in late 1974 the swing-winged B-1A is designed to provide the U.S. Air Force with a versatile weapon covering a wide spectrum of roles. The B-1 designation was assigned to the new bomber as a result of a change of military aircraft classification in 1962. At this time all U.S. military planes were classed under a simple letter/number designation and several high-number categories were started at -1 again. This resulted in some redesignations, especially to Naval aircraft, but in the bomber category no existing types were affected. However, the first new "B" design to follow the XB-70 was destined to become the B-1.

Although considerably smaller than the B-52, the B-1A can carry approximately twice the load of the former at speeds of more than Mach 2. Power for B-1A is in the form of four General Electric F101-GE-100 turbofans. Air is fed to the engines through variable-geometry inlets developed from the XB-70. The nacelles are almost miniatures of the "boat hull" nacelle of the Valkyrie. Each engine develops more than 30,000 lbs.

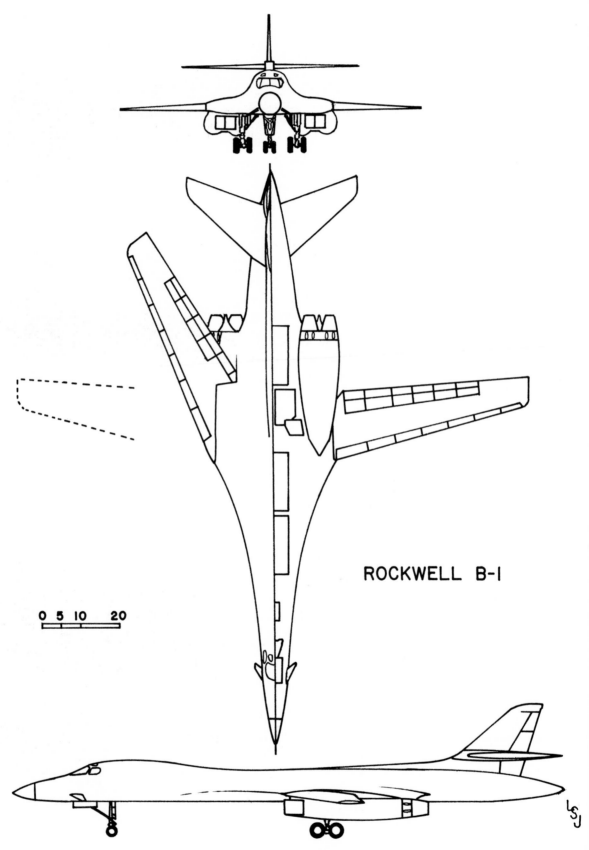

ROCKWELL B-1

0 5 10 20

Fig. 279. Rockwell International B-1.

First B-1A flight test aircraft nears completion early in 1974.

of thrust.

The most unusual feature of the B-1A is its movable wing. For take-off and slow flight the extended wings span 136 feet 8 inches. For supersonic flight the pivoting-wings sweep back from 15 degrees to 65 degrees and a span of 78 feet. In the fully swept configuration the B-1A can exceed Mach 2 at high altitude and Mach 1 for low-level penetration missions. Ground turbulence encountered during high-speed low-level flight can be rough on the crew. To soften the ride a pair of small "canard" vanes are located on the nose. These operate as controls in conjunction with a small section of the three-piece rudder and are activated automatically by sensors which "feel" the turbulence. Inside the cockpit four crewmen carry out their duties in a pressurized "shirt-sleeve" atmosphere similar to the Apollo spacecraft built by

North American. Each pilot has his own fighter-type control stick, wing-sweep actuator and a complete set of throttles.

The B-1 is not fitted with ailerons. Instead, roll is achieved by the use of wing-mounted spoilers working with the horizontal stabilizers.

The use of computers will relieve the crew of much stress. Among these is a system for determining the best power settings for economical cruise and maximum speed. Another computer monitors the fuel and transfers this liquid to various tanks to adjust for CG changes.

The 143 foot long fuselage contains three weapons bays capable of holding 24 Short Range Attack Missiles (SRAM) or a combination of nuclear or high-explosive bombs. In addition, two wing hard points can carry several SRAM's or auxiliary fuel tanks.

Simulated flight view of B-1 mock-up.

APPENDIX

PHOTO GALLERY

244

B-17E model of the Flying Fortress.

YB-17 Fortress prepares for take-off.

The B-18A bomber development of the famous DC-3 airliner.

Douglas B-18A in wartime drab paint.

Allison-powered XB-19A, for years the world's largest plane.

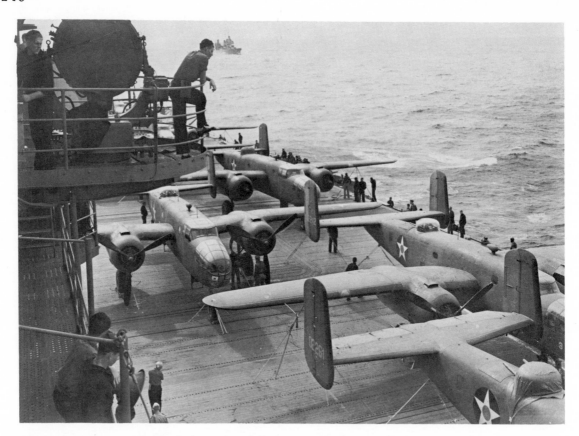

The Doolittle Raiders on board the U.S.S. Hornet before their Tokyo raid.

A Doolittle Raider starts its take-off roll on the Hornet.

B-29 carrying Bell X-1A for air launch.

"Bones", 1,000th B-25H on a bombing mission over Burma.

248

Convair TB-32 Dominator crew trainer.

ID training picture of B-32. Note national insignia has been deleted.

Lockheed-Vega XB-38.

Detail view of XB-38's Allison engines.

A study in aerodynamic simplicity, convair's graceful XB-46.

North American B-45A Tornados.

Turboprop XB-47D test bed.

Composite-powered XB-47D.

Martin XB-51 attack bomber.

The Dart-like B-47 Stratojet.

Boeing B-50D-95.

SAC B-52 with Hound Dog missiles.

B-52 unloads its lethal payload over Vietnam.

The RB-57F is a long-winged four engined development of the Martin Intruder.

The Convair B-58 Hustler carried its nuclear punch in a pod slung underneath.

B-66 on landing roll.

B-66, USAF version of Navy A-3 Skywarrior.

Proposed supersonic transport version of the B-58 Hustler.

Bomber of the future? Convair design study for a nuclear-powered bomber.

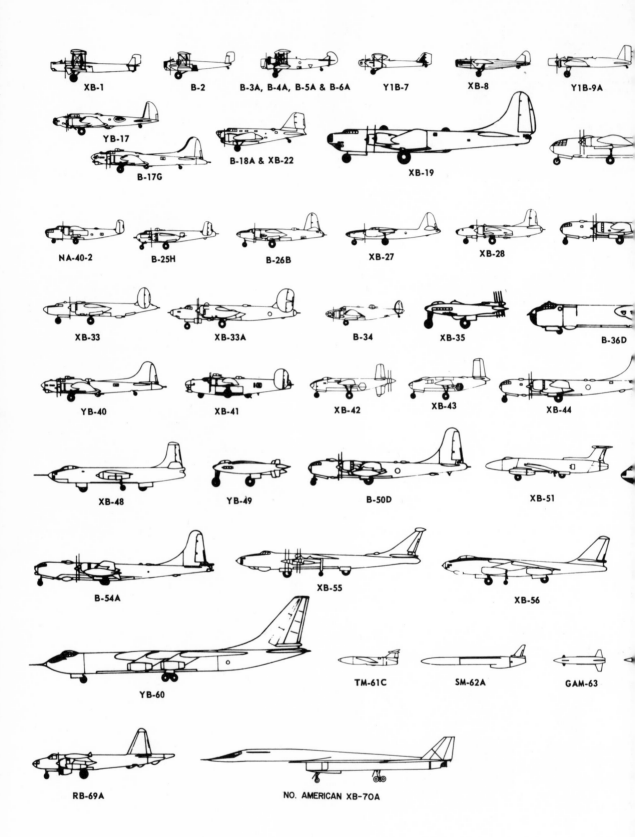

XB-1 B-2 B-3A, B-4A, B-5A & B-6A Y1B-7 XB-8 Y1B-9A

YB-17 B-18A & XB-22 XB-19

B-17G

NA-40-2 B-25H B-26B XB-27 XB-28

XB-33 XB-33A B-34 XB-35 B-36D

YB-40 XB-41 XB-42 XB-43 XB-44

XB-48 YB-49 B-50D XB-51

B-54A XB-55 XB-56

YB-60 TM-61C SM-62A GAM-63

RB-69A NO. AMERICAN XB-70A